WINDY DRYDEN was born in London in 1950. He has worked in psychotherapy and counselling for over twenty-five years, and is the author or editor of over 120 books, including *How to Accept Yourself* (Sheldon Press, 1999) and *Ten Steps to Positive Living* (Sheldon Press, 1994). Dr Dryden is Professor of Counselling at Goldsmiths College, University of London.

Overcoming Common Problems Series

For a full list of titles please contact
Sheldon Press, Marylebone Road, London NW1 4DU

Overcoming Common Problems Series

Overcoming Common Problems Series

Overcoming Common Problems

Overcoming Anxiety

Dr Windy Dryden

Published in Great Britain in 2000
Sheldon Press
Holy Trinity Church
Marylebone Road
London NW1 4DU

British Library Cataloguing-in-Publication Data

A catalogue record for this book is available
from the British Library

ISBN 0–85969–811–5

Typeset by Deltatype Limited, Birkenhead, Merseyside
Printed in Great Britain by
Biddles Ltd, Guildford and King's Lynn

Contents

Preface

This book is part of a developing project of self-help books, each one devoted to a particular emotional problem. Thus, I have written books on overcoming guilt, anger, shame and jealousy and plan to write similar books on overcoming depression, envy and hurt. Without wishing to blow my own trumpet, the books that I have already written for Sheldon Press were fairly easy for me to put together. I would review the most important professional writings in the area, select appropriate client cases from my casebook to discuss (always with their permission and always heavily disguised), develop a sensible structure for the book and get down to the business of putting pen to paper or, to be more accurate, finger to keyboard. This book on overcoming anxiety has caused me far more trouble, however. I've even been tempted to procrastinate on it, which for me is saying something as I rarely procrastinate on my writings, particularly on my self-help writings for Sheldon Press which I greatly enjoy producing.

So why have I had so much difficulty working on this book *Overcoming Anxiety*? Is it because I suffer from anxiety myself and I find the material too painful to write about (a commonly held view in my field to explain unplanned delay)? Or is it because I've suddenly become lazy in my old age and enjoy lounging around rather than getting down to the disciplined business of researching, planning, structuring and writing a book? Actually, neither of these explanations for the difficulty I have had writing this book is correct. First, I do not suffer unduly from anxiety and when I do make myself anxious, normally about my health, I fairly quickly make myself unanxious. And second, one of my strengths as a person, namely my self-discipline, is still intact and I still rarely put off things that are in my interest to do. No, the reason that I have had so much difficulty in writing this book on overcoming anxiety is simply that the subject of anxiety and how to overcome it is vast and complex, and I reluctantly had to conclude that within the constraints of a short, accessible self-help book, I couldn't be as comprehensive in my coverage as I would have liked. Once I accepted this grim fact, without of course liking it (which as I will show you in due course is one important way of overcoming anxiety), I was able to focus on what I could do in this book rather than on what I couldn't. The physician healed himself or, to be strictly accurate, the counsellor counselled himself.

Why am I telling you all this? I am doing so for two reasons: first, I have come to believe in the value of trying to develop a connection with you, my reader, and what better way of doing so than by letting you know something of the trials and tribulations (as well as the joys) of writing; and second, because I hold that one of the keys to overcoming anxiety is being honest with oneself and with others. Attempting to conceal negative features about oneself to oneself and to others, particularly when you try to do this in a desperate way, is likely to lead to anxiety.

Let me tell you, therefore, what I aim to do in this book and what I am not going to do. I have two basic aims in writing this book. My first aim is to discuss the main beliefs that underpin much anxiety and show you how to identify, challenge and, most importantly, change these beliefs to those which will render you far less vulnerable to anxiety. My second aim is to discuss the major ways in which people unwittingly maintain their anxiety, often in subtle ways. I will help you look for your own individual ways of perpetuating your own anxiety and, again most importantly, show you what you can do to tackle these anxiety-maintaining factors.

As I have already mentioned, the field of anxiety is immense and complicated and I will not attempt to do justice to its vast complexity. Thus, I will not discuss the physiology and biochemistry of anxiety. I will not review the evidence concerning to what extent anxiety is inherited and I will not consider the role that medication has in the treatment of anxiety disorders. As with all my books, I am writing this one for those of you who have anxiety which limits your life but does not incapacitate you. If the latter is the case, I strongly suggest that you consult your general practitioner, who will recommend the appropriate course of help which may well be a combination of therapy and medication.

Also, if you have seriously tried to put into practice the principles that I will cover in this book and these have made no difference to you, then again see your GP. It may be that you need some medication to help you to benefit from the ideas presented in this book, or it may be that you need to work face-to-face with a counsellor or therapist who will help you to pinpoint and deal with the individual and specific factors that underpin your anxiety. Self-help books like this one can be enormously useful in helping you to understand and deal with anxiety feelings, and you may help yourself considerably by applying the ideas herein to your individual situation, but they have their limits. You cannot interact with a book or ask it questions. And similarly, a self-help book cannot interact with you and ask you questions to help clarify precisely what is going on when you are anxious. So, if you benefit from this book, that's great and I would be delighted, but if you don't benefit, don't despair. It may be that you need more individualized help than I can give you. Again, see your family doctor as the first port of call if this is the case.

A word on terminology

As I have mentioned in several of my books for Sheldon Press, while words for commonly experienced emotions like anxiety are in everyday use and we think that we all understand what they mean, they are in fact used in different ways by different people. In particular, it is a feature of the approach to counselling and psychotherapy that I practise and which forms the basis for this book – Rational Emotive Behaviour Therapy – to distinguish between healthy and unhealthy negative emotions. I will follow this tradition in this book and distinguish between anxiety which is largely unhealthy and self-defeating and anxiety which is largely healthy and self-enhancing. I thought about referring to the first type of anxiety as unhealthy anxiety or debilitating anxiety and to the second as healthy anxiety or facilitating anxiety, but this proved to be unwieldy, so I finally settled on the following. When I discuss anxiety which is largely unhealthy and self-defeating, I will call this *anxiety* and when I discuss anxiety which is largely healthy and self-enhancing I will call this *concern*. I have no objection if you wish to use your own language to distinguish between the different types of anxiety. Indeed, I encourage you to do so. I sometimes joke with my clients that if they wish to refer to unhealthy anxiety as 'fish' and healthy anxiety as 'chips' that's OK with me. The important thing is you do distinguish between the two types of anxiety and that you make the appropriate translations in your head when you come across my usage of the terms 'anxiety' and 'concern'.

Let me stress one important point at the outset. Concern (or healthy anxiety) is not necessarily a less intense emotion than anxiety (or unhealthy anxiety). It is possible for you to be intensely concerned about something without being anxious about it and without this level of concern interfering with constructive problem-solving and adjustment (depending upon which activity is appropriate to the situation you are facing). Indeed, strong concern will help you in two ways. First, it will alert you to the existence and the nature of the realistic threat you are facing and will help you to deal with it productively. Consequently, when I discuss how you can overcome your (unhealthy) anxiety, I will help you instead to be appropriately (and healthily) concerned about the situations in which you face a realistic threat. Thus, I will not help you to be calm or indifferent about the realistic threats that you will encounter in life. I will not do so because calmness and indifference are not appropriate responses to such threats, in that they do not mobilize you to deal constructively with them. Anxiety mobilizes you, sure enough, but does not do so in ways that are constructive, as I will discuss presently.

Now that I have clarified the terminology that I will be using throughout this book (anxiety vs concern) and that I have set as my goal to help you to be healthily concerned rather than unhealthily anxious when facing threat, let me make one more point before going on to discuss in greater detail the nature of (unhealthy) anxiety in Chapter 1.

Anxiety, not anxiety disorders

In keeping with the general focus of my self-help books for Sheldon Press, I will be writing for those of you whose lives are disadvantaged by anxiety rather than seriously handicapped by it. I will focus on a number of anxiety problems, but I will not deal with situations where these problems are blighting your life – where anxiety has become an anxiety disorder, if you will. This is not to say that if you are suffering from an anxiety disorder then you will not get anything from this book. Far from it. It is just that you need more help than I can give you in the context of a self-help book. So, if your life is handicapped or blighted rather than disadvantaged by anxiety, then please make an appointment to see your doctor, who will arrange appropriate specialist help for you.

Windy Dryden
London & East Sussex

xii

1

The Nature of Anxiety

In this chapter, I will discuss the main components of anxiety. Although these components interact with one another, I will consider them one at a time. But first let me give you a general overview of these components. When you feel (unhealthily) anxious, you are likely to be most aware of the symptoms of anxiety. As you will see, these symptoms can involve your thoughts and images and a variety of bodily sensations and physiological responses. Other than the symptoms of anxiety, several other factors come into play when you are anxious. Thus, you bring to a situation in which you feel anxious a pre-formed, general anxiety-related belief that renders you vulnerable to anxiety. You consider (or make an inference) that you are facing or are about to face some kind of threat (whether this is realistic or not, and in anxiety it is often unrealistic). You hold a specific belief about this threat that is usually a concrete form of the general anxiety-related belief that you brought to this situation. This specific anxiety-related belief has an important impact on your subsequent thinking (including what you pay attention to) and on the way that you behave. Furthermore, your behaviour has consequences. Thus, the way you behave can elicit a response from your environment and in particular from the people in that environment which you may well interpret in ways that maintain your anxiety.

Let me now deal with these components one at a time.

The symptoms of anxiety

When you feel anxious, you are likely to experience your anxiety in a number of different ways which I will present in Table 1. Before I do, I want to stress that it is unlikely that you will experience all of the following symptoms, since different people experience anxiety in different ways.

Table 1   Common symptoms of anxiety.

Breathing and chest	Skeletal/muscular	Sleep
Rapid breathing	Shaking	Difficulty falling asleep
Breathlessness	Trembling	Waking in the night
Tightness in chest	Teeth grinding	Early waking
Chest pains	Eye twitching/blinking	Tossing and turning
Sighing	Wobbly legs	Nightmares
	Tension headaches	

Skin	Mouth and throat	Balance/ear/eye
Sweating	Difficulty swallowing	Loss of balance
Skin reddening	Dry mouth	Spinning sensation
Skin blanching	Lump in throat	Blurred vision
Hot and cold flushes		Ringing in ears
Cold clamminess		Dizziness
Picking at skin		

Intestinal	Speech	Other bodily symptoms
Nausea	Stammering	Tingling
Vomiting	Rapid speech	Numbness
Loss of appetite	Loss of voice	Aches and pains
Stomach churning		Tension

Cardiovascular	Urinary and excretory	Mental symptoms
Heart racing/pounding	Diarrhoea	Difficulty concentrating
Palpitations	Frequent urination	Difficulty thinking
Irregular heartbeat	Urge to defecate	Unable to dismiss certain
Throbbing	Urge to urinate	thoughts
A feeling of faintness	Constipation	'Feeling' world is unreal
Raised blood pressure		'Feeling' self is unreal
(but not detected)		Lack of feeling
Lowered blood pressure		
(in blood and injury		
anxieties, accompanied		
by fainting)		

General anxiety-related beliefs

You are not a blank screen when you face a specific situation. Rather, you bring one or more general beliefs to a situation and these beliefs have a marked influence on whether you are likely to feel unhealthily anxious, healthily concerned or indifferent in the situation. More often than not, you hold these beliefs at an implicit level (which means that these beliefs are below the level of conscious awareness, but can be identified if you know what you are looking for). I will help you to do this at various points throughout this book.

In this section, I will concentrate on general beliefs that tend to underpin anxiety, while in Chapter 2 I will discuss general beliefs that underpin concern. I will only discuss general indifference-related beliefs insofar as they offer an attractive, but ultimately unworkable alternative to general anxiety-related beliefs. This means that my approach is to encourage you to adopt several beliefs that lead to concern rather than those which lead to anxiety.

How can you recognize an anxiety-related belief that is general in nature? You can do so by understanding that it has two main components. First, it has a theme that is likely to span a number of situations (e.g. being in control over your feelings, gaining approval from significant others, doing well at important tasks, being certain that a health-related symptom is benign). Second, the nature of the belief is that it is rigid and extreme. Since rigid and extreme (general and specific beliefs) are at the very core of anxiety, as Albert Ellis, the founder of Rational Emotive Behaviour Therapy, has shown in his voluminous writings over the past forty-five years, they warrant careful explanation and discussion.

General anxiety-related beliefs are rigid and extreme

As my mentor, Albert Ellis, has shown and as I have myself described in my books for Sheldon Press, human beings are disturbed not by things, but by their rigid and extreme beliefs that they hold about things, and this is particularly true when we consider anxiety. The theory of Rational Emotive Behaviour Therapy (REBT) states that these rigid and extreme beliefs are known as irrational beliefs, but as the term 'irrational' has negative connotations for many people, I will refer to them in this book as unhealthy beliefs. There are four unhealthy beliefs that REBT particularly highlights when considering anxiety (and other emotional disorders). The first, and some REBT therapists such as Albert Ellis would say the most important, is rigid and is known as a *demanding belief* which takes the form of a must, absolute should, have to, got to, etc. The other three are extreme and are known as *awfulizing beliefs* (e.g. 'It is awful that . . .', 'It is terrible that . . .' or 'It is the end of the world that . . .'), *low frustration tolerance (LFT) beliefs* (e.g. 'I can't bear it when . . .', 'I couldn't stand it if . . .' or 'It would be intolerable to me if . . .') and *depreciation beliefs* (e.g. 'I would be worthless if . . .', 'You would be worthless if . . .' or 'The world would be a rotten place if . . .'). Let us take a closer look at these four unhealthy beliefs and see how they underpin anxiety.

Demanding beliefs

Brian regularly became anxious before giving presentations at work. His general anxiety-related belief contained a demanding belief as follows: 'I absolutely have to come across well to my peers and to my boss.' As you can see, this belief contains both a theme, 'coming across well to my peers and to my boss', and a rigid, demanding belief about this theme, 'I absolutely have to . . .' The problem with demanding beliefs such as Brian's is that they are false, illogical and, perhaps most importantly, they have disturbed consequences.

Why are demanding beliefs false? Well, when you make a demand about yourself, others and/or life conditions, you hold that you, others and life conditions literally have to be a certain way. Now, if there was a law of the universe (or a law of nature) which decreed, for example, that Brian must come across well to his peers and to his boss, then there would be no way that he could possibly come across in any other way to them but well. It would not be possible, therefore, if Brian's demanding belief were true, for him to come across poorly to them or even averagely to them, because such events would be prevented from happening by the law of the universe (or nature) which states 'Brian must come across well to his peers and to his boss'. Interestingly enough, if Brian's demanding belief were true, it would not be possible for Brian to come across poorly to his peers and to his boss, even if he was determined to do a poor job in front of them, since the law of the universe would stop him from doing so.

So demanding beliefs are rarely, if ever, true, and when you hold such a belief you are insisting that you, others and life conditions that are the focus of your belief have to be the way that you insist they should be. However, even when you try as hard as you can to exclude the possibility that a particular outcome will happen, the world does not change to satisfy your demand. Thus, Brian cannot exclude the possibility that he may come across averagely or even poorly to his peers and to his boss, no matter how hard he demands that these outcomes must not happen. The only way that you can make your demands come true is by running the universe and by making the world in your God-like image. Lots of luck. If you ever make it, however, please call on me because I would like a full head of hair and I'm sure that you will make time to fulfil my desire!

Why are demanding beliefs illogical? Essentially, because they attempt to derive a rigidity from what is essentially flexible. When you hold a rigid, demanding belief, most of the time this belief is a rigid version of a belief that is flexible. Thus, Brian's rigid belief: 'I must come across well to my peers and to my boss' is based on his non-rigid preference: 'I want to come across well to my peers and to my boss.' Brian's demanding belief can for our purposes be expressed thus: 'Because I want to come across well to my peers and to my boss [non-rigid], therefore I must come across well to them [rigid].' As philosophers will tell you, you cannot logically derive something that is rigid from something that is non-rigid. Thus, demanding beliefs are illogical because they attempt to derive a rigid view from one that is non-rigid.

Finally, why are demanding beliefs largely unconstructive? Because they very frequently lead to anxious feelings, anxious thinking and anxious behaviour. When Brian demands that he must come over well to his peers and to his boss and he acknowledges to himself that this might not happen, then he is anxious about this eventuality, largely because his demand has made this something that he must not experience. Anxiety is frequently the result when there is a conflict between what is (or may be) and what must be, when these are radically different and when you think that 'what may be' is likely to happen. Thus, for Brian, what may be is that he may fail to come across well to his peers and to his boss, whereas what must be is that he must come across well to them. When these very different scenarios conflict, and when 'what may be' is deemed likely to occur, anxiety is frequently the result.

In addition, demanding beliefs frequently lead to anxious thoughts and anxiety-related behaviour. Thus, when Brian sees that he may not come across well to his peers and to his boss and believes that he must come across well to them, then he is likely to engage in anxious thinking such as 'They will all hate what I have to say', 'They will think that I am an idiot' and 'I won't get my bonus at the end of the year.' These thoughts elaborate and exacerbate the threat that he thinks he is facing. Furthermore, demanding beliefs frequently lead to anxiety-related behaviour. Thus, when Brian sees that he may not come across well to his peers and to his boss and believes that he must come across well to them, then he is likely to stumble over his words or speak too quickly, he may refrain from engaging in appropriate eye contact with his audience or he may feign illness and cancel his presentation. As you can see, then, demanding beliefs can have a profound detrimental effect on a person's psychological state and functioning.

Awfulizing beliefs

As we have seen, Brian regularly became anxious before giving presentations at work. His general anxiety-related belief also contained an awfulizing belief as follows: 'It would be awful if I did not come across well to my peers and to my boss.' As you can see, this belief contains both a theme, 'not coming across well to my peers and to my boss', and an extreme awfulizing belief about this theme: 'It would be awful if . . .' The problem with awfulizing beliefs such as Brian's is that they are again false, illogical and they have disturbed consequences.

Why are awfulizing beliefs false? First, they are false because they imply that nothing can be worse. If it were true that not coming across well to his peers and to his boss was awful for Brian then nothing worse could possibly happen to him. A moment's reflection reveals this to be utterly false. I am fond of quoting the mother of Smokey Robinson, the famous Tamla Motown singer in this regard. She was reported to have told her son: 'From the day you were born till you ride in the hearse, there's nothing so bad that it couldn't be worse!'

Second, awfulizing beliefs are false because they imply that whatever is deemed to be 'awful' is really more than 100 per cent bad. Albert Ellis has said that 'awful' in this sense stems from the demand that 'this bad thing must not be as bad as it is'. Well, even if Brian could prove that not coming over well to his peers and to his boss was 100 per cent bad and that therefore nothing could be worse (which, as I have shown above, he really can't), how can he possibly prove the truth of the proposition that this eventuality is more than 100 per cent? The answer is, of course, that he can't. The idea that something can be more than 100 per cent bad is preposterous, since 100 per cent bad already means that nothing can be worse.

The third reason why awfulizing beliefs are false is that they imply that no good can possibly come from the situation (or situations) being evaluated as 'awful'. Can Brian really prove that if he does not come across well to his peers and to his boss, nothing good can come of this? Of course he can't. In fact, he can prove that something good can come of it. For example, between 1983 and 1985, I applied for 54 jobs and failed to get any of them. What good came out of this for me? A number of things. First, I learned that I could cope in the face of adversity. Thus, as I am fond of saying, I had 54 job rejections and 0 self-rejections in that I did not depreciate myself at all for my 'failures'. I did not know that I could do this until I was faced with this ongoing state of affairs. Second, I learned from the feedback I sought that what I regarded as my confidence was being perceived as arrogance and was turning off potential employers. I took this very much on board, thought carefully about how I was presenting myself, decided to change aspects of my behaviour and was soon successful at finding a new job. I maintain that two very good things came out of the bad situation of failing to get any of the 54 jobs that I applied for, and if this was true for me why couldn't good things (as well as, of course, bad things) come from Brian not coming across well to his peers and to his boss? The answer is that they definitely can.

In conclusion, awfulizing beliefs are false in that you can prove (1) that things can almost always be worse than what you are evaluating as 'awful'; (2) that the concept of something being more than 100 per cent is magical, and (3) you can almost always derive some good from even the most tragic of circumstances. In saying all of this, I am not belittling or making light of tragedies, holocausts and the like. My goal is to help you to take the 'awfulness' (as carefully defined here) out of tragedy, not to help you to take the tragedy out of tragedy.

Why are awfulizing beliefs illogical? Essentially, because they attempt to derive something extreme from something non-extreme. When you hold an extreme awfulizing belief, most of the time this belief is an extreme version of a belief that is non-extreme. Thus, Brian's extreme awfulizing belief, 'It would be awful if I did not come across well to my peers and to my boss', is based on a non-extreme version of this belief: 'It would be bad if I did not come across well to my peers and to my boss.' Brian's awfulizing belief can, for our purposes, be expressed thus: 'Because it would be bad if I did not come across well to my boss [non-extreme], therefore it would be awful if this happened [extreme].' Again, philosophers will tell you that you cannot logically derive something that is extreme from something that is non-extreme. Thus, awfulizing beliefs are illogical because they attempt to derive an extreme view from one that is non-extreme.

Finally, why are awfulizing beliefs largely unconstructive? For the same reason that demanding beliefs are predominantly unconstructive: because they very frequently lead to anxious feelings, anxious thinking and anxious behaviour. When Brian holds that it would be awful if he did not come over well to his peers and to his boss and he acknowledges to himself that this might happen, then he is anxious about this eventuality because he is giving it an extremely negative evaluation. Anxiety is frequently the result when you think that something bad may happen and you believe that it would be awful, terrible or the end of the world were it to happen. Some people call awfulizing 'horrorizing' to emphasize this.

Awfulizing does not only lead you to experiencing anxious feelings, it also frequently leads to anxious thoughts and anxiety-related behaviour. Thus, when Brian sees that he may not come across well to his peers and to his boss and believes that it would be awful if this happened, then he is likely to engage in thinking which is consistent with 'horror'. Thus, he may think that people will heckle him or leave the room in droves. He may think that failing to come across well to his peers and to his boss may end his career and that no-one will ever employ him again. If he goes this far, he may then, in his mind's eye, picture himself being destitute and on the streets. I hope you can see that these extremely negative scenarios are consistent with the horror made explicit in awfulizing beliefs.

Furthermore, awfulizing beliefs frequently lead to anxiety-related behaviour. Thus, when Brian sees that he may not come across well to his peers and to his boss and believes that it would be awful if that happened, then he is likely to act in ways that are very similar to how he would act when he held a demanding belief in such situations (e.g. stumbling over his words or speaking too quickly, not engaging in appropriate eye contact with his audience or avoiding making the presentation). Like demanding beliefs, awfulizing beliefs have a profound detrimental effect on a person's psychological state and functioning.

Low frustration tolerance (LFT) beliefs

By now, you will know that Brian regularly became anxious before giving presentations at work. His general anxiety-related belief also contained a low frustration tolerance (LFT) belief as follows: 'I couldn't bear it if I did not come across well to my peers and to my boss.' As you can see, this belief contains both a theme, 'not coming across well to my peers and to my boss', and an extreme LFT belief about this theme, 'I couldn't bear it if . . .' Once again, the problem with LFT beliefs such as Brian's is that they are false, illogical and have disturbed consequences.

Why are LFT beliefs false? Because they do not correspond to reality. If it were true that Brian couldn't bear it if he failed to come across well to his peers and to his boss, one of two things would happen. Either he would disintegrate and die or he would lose the capacity to experience happiness in the future, no matter how he thought about not coming across well to his peers and to his boss. A moment's reflection leads to the conclusion that neither of these situations will, in all probability, occur. Let's suppose that I gave Brian the following choice: he could save the life of his children by not coming across well to his peers and to his boss, or he could come across well to his boss and to his peers by sacrificing the lives of his children. Which option do you think he would choose? In all probability, he would select the first. This proves that the idea that Brian can't bear not coming across well to his peers and to his boss is false. He can bear this, and particularly so if it is worth tolerating.

In conclusion, LFT beliefs are false in that you can prove that you will not disintegrate or die if you face negative events that are truly not life-threatening, and that you will not lose the capacity to experience happiness in such circumstances and, in all probability, will indeed experience happiness and pleasure in the future. Again, in saying this, I am not belittling or making light of tragedies, holocausts and the like. My goal is to help you to see, however, that you can bear what you think you cannot bear, particularly if you see that doing so has a purpose. People can and do transcend the worst of situations and can grow from the experience. They rarely do this without a lot of pain and struggle, but it is possible for them – and you – to do so.

Why are LFT beliefs illogical? As with awfulizing beliefs, because they attempt to derive something extreme from something non-extreme. When you hold an extreme LFT belief, most of the time this belief is an extreme version of a belief that is non-extreme. Thus, Brian's extreme LFT belief, 'I wouldn't be able to bear it if I did not come across well to my peers and to my boss', is based on a non-extreme version of this belief: 'I would find it difficult to bear if I did not come across well to my peers and to my boss.' Brian's LFT belief can, for our purposes, be expressed thus: 'Because I would find it difficult to bear if I did not come across well to my peers and to my boss [non-extreme], therefore it would be unbearable if this happened [extreme].' Once again, you cannot logically derive something that is extreme from something that is non-extreme. Thus, LFT beliefs (like awfulizing beliefs) are illogical because they attempt to derive an extreme view from one that is non-extreme.

Finally, why are LFT beliefs largely unconstructive? Because, like demanding and awfulizing beliefs, they lead to anxious feelings, anxious thinking and anxious behaviour. Thus, when Brian holds that he would not be able to bear it if he did not come over well to his peers and to his boss and he acknowledges to himself that this might happen, then he is anxious about this eventuality because of his perceived inability to deal with the situation. If anyone thinks that they will, in effect, disintegrate in the face of threat, then anxiety occurs if the person thinks that the threat is imminent.

As I said above, holding LFT beliefs also leads to anxious thinking. Thus, when Brian sees that he may not come across well to his peers and to his boss and believes that he would not be able to bear it if this happened, then he is likely to engage in thinking which is consistent with his perceived inability to tolerate the event. Thus, he may think that he would lose control of himself if he remained in the situation. For example, he may predict that he would get very anxious and that those present would easily detect his loss of emotional control.

I am sometimes asked whether LFT beliefs are really the same as awfulizing beliefs. My reply is that they are similar, but differ in one or two key respects. Thus, when you hold predominantly an awfulizing belief (as opposed to an LFT belief), you focus more on the 'horrors' of the world ('*It* would be awful if . . .'), whereas when you hold predominantly an LFT belief (as opposed to an awfulizing belief), you focus more on the internal 'horrors' (in Brian's case '*I* would not be able to bear it if . . .'). In this respect, I would expect the content of thinking stemming from LFT beliefs to reflect this greater internal focus (here, Brian's thinking focuses on his possible loss of control) as compared with the greater external focus in thinking stemming from awfulizing beliefs (here, Brian's thinking focuses on the behaviour of others present, e.g. that people will heckle him or leave the room in droves).

As already noted, LFT beliefs frequently lead to anxiety-related behaviour. Thus, when Brian sees that he may not come across well to his peers and to his boss and believes that he would not be able to bear it if this happened, then he is likely to act in ways that are very similar to how he would act when he held a demanding belief or an awfulizing belief in such situations. Thus, he would do everything that he could to get out of giving presentations at work, but if he couldn't do so then he would stumble over his words or speak too quickly or not engage in appropriate eye contact with his audience during the presentation. Like demanding beliefs and awfulizing beliefs, LFT beliefs have a profound detrimental effect on a person's psychological state and functioning.

Depreciation beliefs

As I will discuss later in this book, there are two major types of (unhealthy) anxiety: ego anxiety and non-ego anxiety. Both types of anxiety are based on all four unhealthy beliefs outlined on pp. 3–4 (i.e. demanding beliefs, awfulizing beliefs, LFT beliefs and depreciation beliefs). Where they differ is with respect to the kind of depreciation beliefs being held. When your anxiety is ego-based then your depreciation beliefs are about yourself; I will call these beliefs self-depreciation beliefs throughout this book. However, when your anxiety is non-ego based, then your depreciation beliefs are about others or about the world or life conditions. In this section, I will consider depreciation beliefs with reference to self-depreciation beliefs, but what I have to say also applies to depreciation beliefs about others and about the world/life conditions.

Let us now return to Brian who, as you will remember, regularly became anxious before giving presentations at work. His general anxiety-related belief contained a self-depreciation belief as follows: 'If I do not come across well to my peers and to my boss, this will prove that I am an inadequate person.' As you can see, this belief contains both a theme, 'not coming across well to my peers and to my boss', and an extreme belief about Brian in relation to this theme: 'I am an inadequate person.' As with demanding beliefs, awfulizing beliefs and LFT beliefs, the problem with self-depreciation beliefs such as Brian's is that they are false, illogical and once again they have disturbed consequences.

Why are self-depreciation beliefs false? Well, when you depreciate yourself, you are saying, in effect, that your entire 'self' is inadequate. Now, if it were true that you were inadequate, then everything about you would be inadequate and that would also hold for your past and your future. This is very, very unlikely. As my colleague, Dr Paul Hauck, showed in his book *Hold Your Head Up High* (Sheldon, 1991), your 'self' is 'every conceivable thing about you that can be rated'. Since this involves your thoughts, emotions, behaviours, etc., it soon becomes apparent that your 'self' is incredibly complex. A rating such as 'inadequate' applied to your 'self', on the other hand, implies that your 'self' is simple. If you were a single-cell amoeba and that single cell was inadequate, then your self-depreciation belief, 'I am inadequate', would be true. Applied to a complex human being like yourself, then, it is clearly false. In addition, you are constantly changing as a human being and thus, even if it were true that you were inadequate up to this present moment, you would have to continue being inadequate in all respects until the moment that you die for the self-depreciation belief 'I am inadequate' to be true.

Why are self-depreciation beliefs illogical? Essentially, because when you hold such a belief, you are making what philosophers call the part–whole error. Thus, Brian is making the part–whole error when he concludes that he, as a person, is inadequate [whole] on the basis of him not coming across well to his peers and to his boss [part]. If Brian was a single-cell amoeba whose only characteristic was 'not coming across well to his peers and to his boss', then it would be logical for him to conclude that he was inadequate as a person. But Brian is a complex human being with millions upon millions of parts, and therefore it is illogical to define his totality on the basis of one of those millions upon millions of parts. In this way, self-depreciation beliefs (and beliefs which depreciate others and the world/life conditions) are illogical in that they all make the (illogical) part–whole error.

Finally, why are self-depreciation beliefs largely unconstructive? Yes, you've guessed it: because they very frequently lead to anxious feelings, anxious thinking and anxious behaviour. When Brian acknowledges to himself that he might not come over well to his peers and his boss and he considers himself to be an inadequate person if this happens, then he will make himself anxious about events where this may happen. Self-depreciation beliefs (and the demanding beliefs that underpin or are closely linked with them) are at the root of much ego anxiety (i.e. anxiety concerning threats to self-esteem).

Self-depreciation beliefs, when activated, frequently lead to anxious thoughts and anxiety-related behaviour. Thus, when Brian sees that he may not come across well to his peers and to his boss and believes that he is an inadequate person if this happens, then he is likely to engage in anxious thinking that tends to emphasize his other inadequacies (internal ego focus) and others' negative views of these inadequacies (external focus). He may also see himself (either in thought or in image) in situations which are likely (given his self-depreciation beliefs) to lead to him experiencing shame or humiliation. Thus, once he is anxious he may think that others may laugh at him or 'show him up' in large gatherings. Once again, these thoughts elaborate and exacerbate the threat that he thinks he is facing.

Finally, self-depreciation beliefs frequently lead to anxiety-related behaviour. Thus, when Brian sees that he may not come across well to his peers and to his boss and believes that he is an inadequate person if this happens, then he will do his best to avoid such threatening situations, or if he can't, he will display behavioural manifestations of anxiety like stumbling over his words, speaking too quickly or refraining from engaging in appropriate eye contact with his audience. Once again, self-depreciation beliefs can have a profound detrimental effect on a person's psychological state.

Threat: what you feel anxious about

Brian has a colleague, Mike, with whom he works closely. One morning, Brian and Mike were told that the following week they would have to make a presentation to the rest of the company (including their boss) on a project they were working on together with a third colleague, Graham. Brian immediately felt anxious while Mike did not. Why did Brian react to this news with anxiety while Mike took it in his stride? For two reasons. First, Brian experienced the news that he and Mike had to present their work to their peers and to their boss as a threat, and Mike did not. And second, Brian held a specific anxiety-related belief about this specific event and Mike did not. This last point is revealing. If you do not consider that you are under threat then it is very unlikely that you will hold a specific anxiety-related belief and thus you will not feel anxiety. Let me show, in diagrammatic form, Brian's and Mike's different reactions to the news that they had to present their ideas to the whole group in a week's time:

News of the upcoming presentation

Brian: Threat + specific anxiety-related belief = anxiety
Mike: No threat/no specific anxiety-related belief = no anxiety

We now know why Brian felt anxious about the presentation. First, he saw this as a threat and second, he held a specific anxiety-related belief about this threat. I want to stress an important point. Threat is a necessary condition for anxiety to be felt, but it isn't sufficient. As I have just mentioned, Brian and Mike had another colleague, Graham, with whom they worked closely. Graham only found out about the presentation the day before it was to take place, because he had been off sick. When he found out about the presentation, he felt concerned (or healthily anxious) rather than (unhealthily) anxious about it. Graham experienced exactly the same threat as Brian, but held a specific concern-related (rather than anxiety-related) belief about it. I will discuss the nature of concern thoroughly in the next chapter and specific anxiety-related beliefs in the next section of this chapter.

So you have to experience threat to feel anxious or concerned. If you hold anxiety-related beliefs about this threat, you will feel anxious, and if you hold concern-related beliefs about it, then you will feel concerned.

But, you may be thinking, why did Brian find the presentation threatening while Mike did not? The answer is that Brian brought to this situation a general pre-formed anxiety-related belief, which meant that he focused on the threatening aspects of the specific situation that were consistent with the content of his general anxiety-related belief. Since Mike did not hold a general anxiety-related belief the content of which was relevant to the specific situation that both he and Brian faced, he did not experience the situation as threatening.

Let's look more closely at why Brian found the news that he and his team had to make a presentation to his wider group of peers and to his boss threatening. Let me remind you of his salient general anxiety-related belief (for clarity's sake, I will refer only to the demanding and self-depreciation components of this belief): 'I absolutely have to come across well to my peers and to my boss and I am an inadequate person if I don't.' This is a general belief because it does not specify any concrete situations. It points to a general class of events where Brian thinks that he might not come across well to his peers and to his boss. This explains why Brian may not be anxious in all situations where he is performing in front of his peers and his boss. Thus, if he were sure that he would come across well to his peers and to his boss during the presentation in question, then Brian would probably not feel anxious, because he would not 'feel' under threat. But if he suddenly thought that his performance wasn't as good as he predicted and/or that his peers and his boss did not think that he was coming across well, then he would be anxious because he would suddenly consider that he was under threat and he would hold a specific anxiety-related belief about this threat (see next section).

So, unless Brian is very confident that he will come across well to his peers and to his boss, he will find the presentation a threat because he thinks that there is a good chance that he might not come across well during it. It is as if Brian were saying to himself: 'I believe generally that I have to come across well to my peers and to my boss and I will be an inadequate person if I don't. Here is a specific situation where there is a good chance I might not come across well to them. I thus find this situation a threat.'

Mike, on the other hand, as we have seen, does not find this situation threatening because he holds no relevant general anxiety-related belief. He may think that he will come over well to the assembled grouping, he may think that he might not come over well to them and this is not an issue for him, or he does not think about how well or poorly he may perform because he is focused on *what* he is going to do rather than on *how well* (or *poorly*) he may be able to do it.

Putting this diagrammatically once again:

News of the upcoming presentation

Brian: General anxiety-related belief + prediction that there is a good chance that I might not perform well = threat

Brian: General anxiety-related belief + confident that I will perform well = no threat

Mike: No relevant general anxiety-related belief = no threat

Now, if you hold a general anxiety-related belief about a theme (e.g. not coming across well to your peers and to your boss) and you encounter a situation in which this theme may become reality (e.g. giving a specific presentation to your peers and to your boss where it is possible that you may not come across well to them), then this belief will lead you to focus on how poorly you may do in the actual upcoming situation rather than on what you might be saying, and to overestimate the chances that the theme will become a reality in the specific situation under consideration. Thus, because Brian holds the general anxiety-related belief that he must come across well to his peers and to his boss and he would be an inadequate person if he does not, when he is told about the forthcoming presentation (specific situation) where it is possible that he may not come across well to them, then he will focus more on the possibility that he may not come across well on the day rather than on the possibility that he may perform well. Also, whenever he tries to focus on what he might say, he will be drawn back to thinking that he might not say it well.

In summary, when Brian learns about the forthcoming presentation, his general anxiety-related belief leads him to focus on threatening aspects of this situation that are consistent with the content of his belief rather than on aspects of the situation that are inconsistent with this content or are not relevant to it. Let me again put this into diagrammatic form.

Brian's general anxiety-related belief	$\rightarrow$ *Specific event*	$\rightarrow$ *Threat*
I must come across well to my peers and to my boss and I am an inadequate person if I don't.	News of forthcoming presentation to peers and to boss where I may not come across well.	There is a good chance that I will not come across well.

Let me review the points that I have made so far in this section about threat.

1 When we feel anxious (or for that matter concerned), we consider that we are facing some kind of threat.
2 Threat is a necessary, but not sufficient, factor in anxiety. Thus, when we are anxious, a sense of threat is almost always present, but it is our anxiety-related beliefs about this threat that lead us to feel anxious. If we hold a concern-related belief about this threat we will feel concerned rather than anxious.
3 We may have a general anxiety-related belief, but we will not feel anxious until we experience a relevant threat which triggers a specific version of this general belief.
4 We bring our general anxiety-related beliefs (e.g. Brian's belief: 'I must come across well to my peers and to my boss and I am an inadequate person if I don't') to situations, and when we encounter a specific situation where the content of the general belief *may* become reality (e.g. when Brian learns about the forthcoming presentation where he may not come across well), this belief leads us to focus on the relevant threatening aspects of the situation (e.g. Brian focuses on the possibility of not coming across well rather than on coming across well or on what he is going to say).

Two types of threat: ego and non-ego

In 1976, Dr Aaron T. Beck published a book entitled *Cognitive Therapy and the Emotional Disorders*, in which he introduced the concept of the *personal domain*. Our personal domain refers to those people (including ourselves), objects and principles in which we have a personal involvement or investment. These people, objects and principles may occupy a place on the periphery of our personal domain, at a midway point within it or at the very core of it. Generally speaking, given the presence of an anxiety-related belief, when something or someone towards the core of our personal domain is threatened, our feelings of anxiety are more intense than when someone or something occupying a less central (middle or peripheral) position within this domain is threatened.

My own experience in dealing with hundreds of clients with anxiety problems over the years is that people present with anxiety when they experience threats to the two main areas within the personal domain. I will refer to these areas as 'ego' and 'non-ego'. By 'ego', I mean what is popularly termed self-esteem. When you perceive a threat to your ego or self-esteem, you think that something may occur which will lead you to have lowered self-esteem. The anxiety that you experience when you face such a threat can be called ego anxiety and occurs when you experience a threat to your ego and when you hold an anxiety-related belief about this threat. Put diagrammatically, we have:

Threat to ego (or self-esteem) + anxiety-related belief = ego anxiety

What kind of situations can constitute a threat to your ego (or self-esteem)? A great many, but perhaps the most frequent are the anticipation of:

• failure;
• poor performance;
• not being loved/liked;
• being rejected;
• being criticized;
• being disapproved;
• someone whom you value preferring another to you;
• not having something you value which someone else has;
• acting poorly in public;
• failing to achieve your ideal.

What, then is meant by the term 'non-ego'? By 'non-ego', I refer to areas which do not involve your ego or self-esteem. When you perceive a threat to non-ego areas of your personal domain, you think that something may occur which will lead you to be disadvantaged within these areas of your domain. The anxiety that you experience when you face such a threat can be called non-ego anxiety, and occurs when you experience a threat to non-ego areas of your personal domain and when you hold an anxiety-related belief about this threat. Put diagrammatically, we have:

Threat to non-ego + anxiety-related belief = non-ego anxiety

What kind of situations can constitute a threat to non-ego areas of your personal domain? Again, a great many, but perhaps the most frequent are the anticipation of:

- frustration;
- discomfort;
- emotional and/or physical pain;
- non-ego loss;
- unfairness/injustice to self or others;
- loss of control;
- uncertainty;
- illness;
- loss of security;
- physical danger.

To complicate matters, all the threats that I listed under threats to ego may also constitute threats to non-ego areas of your personal domain. However, this issue lies outside the scope of this book.

I want to reiterate a point that I made in the previous section. You are likely to focus on threatening aspects of a situation if you hold a general anxiety-related belief which directs your attention to these features because they are consistent with the content of this general belief. Although I have exemplified this in the case of Brian, discussed above, I will give two more examples, one involving ego threat and one involving non-ego threat.

One of Harriet's ego anxiety-related beliefs is: 'I must be approved by new people that I meet and if I'm not I am not a very nice person.' When she went to a party held by one of her friends, she became anxious when she was introduced to a group of people whom she did not know. Harriet's general ego anxiety-related belief directed her attention to two strangers who did not smile very much when talking to her, which she took as a sign that they did not like her. Harriet focused on the threatening aspects of the situation where she thought that the two strangers did not like her, which was consistent with her general belief that she is not a nice person if people she has just met do not approve of her.

Note that Harriet assumes that the two people she has just met do not like her because they do not smile very much. This is what happens when you hold a general ego anxiety-related belief and bring this to situations which are salient to the content of the belief. Harriet's belief leads her to the assumption that the only way that people can prove to her that they like her is to demonstrate approval, in this case by smiling frequently at her. However, a moment's objective reflection would show Harriet that some people are reserved and do not smile very much. They do not overtly show approval, particularly with people whom they have just met. But the presence of Harriet's general anxiety-related belief means that in situations that are relevant to this belief, she is not going to engage in such objective thinking. I will return to this topic later in the book.

Sarah holds the general non-ego anxiety-related belief as follows: 'I must know for sure that members of my family are safe and it would be terrible if I wasn't sure about their safety.' One evening Jane, Sarah's 21-year-old daughter who still lived at home, was late home from a party. Jane said that she would be home at 10.30 p.m. and at 10.40 p.m. Sarah was frantic with worry. As you will now know, Sarah brings her general non-ego belief to situations where it is possible that she does not know for sure that members of her family are safe. In doing so, Sarah equates uncertainty about the safety of Jane as evidence that Jane is in great danger. Now, there are a number of possibilities here, so let me list the three that are most relevant to show the impact that Jane's general non-ego anxiety-related belief has on what she pays attention to:

1 Jane is ten minutes late and Sarah does not know that she is safe: Jane is safe.
2 Jane is ten minutes late and Sarah does not know that she is safe: Jane is in slight danger.
3 Jane is ten minutes late and Sarah does not know that she is safe: Jane is in great danger.

If we asked a hundred women of Sarah's age and background to select the most probable scenario, my guess is that the vast majority would select Scenario 1. Yet Sarah is convinced that Scenario 3 is true. Why? Because her general non-ego anxiety-related belief leads her to focus on the most threatening (even though least likely) aspect of the situation.

In summary, when you hold a general anxiety-related belief, you

19

bring this belief to a relevant specific situation and this belief leads you to focus on threatening aspects of the situation that are consistent with the content of your general belief.

Specific anxiety-related beliefs

So far, I have discussed anxiety-related beliefs that are general in nature, i.e. which apply to a range of relevant situations. However, anxiety-related beliefs can also be specific in nature and apply to the specific situation in which you find yourself. Let me return to the case of Brian to make clear the distinction between general and specific anxiety-related beliefs. If you recall, the anxiety-related belief that Brian held which has been the focus for discussion was as follows: 'I must come across well to my peers and to my boss and I am an inadequate person if I do not.' This is a general belief because it applies to all relevant situations where Brian considers that he may not come across well to these people. It encompasses the specific situation where Brian was told that he (and his group) would have to make a presentation before his peers and his boss, and it applies to other similar situations as well.

Brian's specific anxiety-related belief that he held about the specific situation under consideration was as follows: 'When I give my presentation next week, I must come across well to my peers and to my boss in this situation and if I don't this proves that I am an inadequate person.' As you can see, Brian's specific anxiety-related belief is a concrete version of his general anxiety-related belief. It differs from the latter in that it specifies the situation that Brian is anxious about (i.e. the specific forthcoming occasion when Brian would have to give an actual presentation).

You will recall that Brian brings his general anxiety-related belief to the specific event and focuses on a threatening aspect of this situation that is consistent with the content of this general belief. This is shown in the diagram below.

General anxiety-related belief (GAB)
('I must come across well to my peers and to my boss')

Relevant specific situation
(Forthcoming presentation)

Focus on threat in this situation (consistent with GAB)
('There is a good chance that I will not come across well
to my peers and to my boss in this presentation')

Then, having focused on this threatening aspect of this specific situation, Brian now appraises this specific threat (rather than the situation itself) with the specific version of his anxiety-related belief (i.e. 'When I give *this* presentation, I must come across well to my peers and to my boss and if I don't this proves that I am an inadequate person'). This is shown in the diagram below.

General anxiety-related belief (GAB)
('I must come across well to my peers and to my boss')

↓

Relevant specific situation
(Forthcoming presentation)

↓

Focus on threat in this situation (consistent with GAB)
('There is a good chance that I will not come across well
to my peers and to my boss in this presentation')

Specific anxiety-related belief
('I must come across well to my peers and to my boss in this
presentation and if I don't then I am an inadequate person')

So, you bring a general anxiety-related belief to a relevant specific situation and in doing so you focus on a threatening aspect of this situation that is consistent with the content of this belief. Then, you appraise this threat with a specific version of your general anxiety-related belief.

You will recall that general anxiety-related beliefs are composed of demands, awfulizing beliefs, LFT beliefs and depreciation beliefs about general situations. Well, specific anxiety-related beliefs are also composed of demands, awfulizing beliefs, LFT beliefs and depreciation beliefs, but these are held about specific situations.

Anxiety and thinking

So far in this chapter, I have argued that thinking plays a central role in anxiety. This sounds relatively straightforward, but it is, in reality, quite complex. Let me try to present this complexity as clearly as I can by referring to REBT's famous ABC framework.

In its simplest form we have the following:

$$A = \text{Activating event}$$
$$B = \text{Belief}$$
$$C = \text{Consequences}$$

Beliefs (B)

Let me start with B because this is the easiest component to understand. In REBT, B stands for beliefs. These are fully evaluative thoughts that underpin our emotions. There are basically two types of beliefs that we may hold about events: healthy and unhealthy. In this chapter, I have concentrated on the unhealthy (general and specific) beliefs which underpin anxiety. These are rigid and extreme and comprise demanding beliefs, awfulizing beliefs, low frustration tolerance (LFT) beliefs and depreciation beliefs. In the next chapter, I will concentrate on the healthy beliefs that underpin concern. As you will see, these are flexible and non-extreme and take the form of full preferences, anti-awfulizing beliefs, high frustration tolerance (HFT) beliefs and acceptance beliefs.

Inferences of threat (at A)

As noted in the simple ABC framework, A stands for 'activating event'. An activating event can be an actual situation (in Brian's case being told that he had to give a presentation to his peers and to his boss in a week's time) or, much more frequently in anxiety, it can be an inference about this event. An inference is a thought and can be best seen as a hunch about the actual situation that goes beyond the data at hand. The inference may be accurate or inaccurate, but more data are needed before the accuracy (or inaccuracy) of this inference can be determined. An example of an inference is the one Brian made about his forthcoming presentation: 'There is a good chance that I will not come across well to my peers and to my boss when I give my presentation next week.' Inferences can be specific (most frequently about specific events, as in the above example) or they can be more general (about more general categories of events).

Often, in anxiety, you have no way of knowing for certain whether an inference is likely to be accurate or inaccurate. The reason for this is that, in anxiety, inferences are very frequently about future events and we have no way of knowing for certain whether future events will happen or not. Given this, we need to go along with the best bet, the most probable eventuality. The trouble is that in anxiety, as we will see, you often select an inference that is consistent with your anxiety-related belief but which is less probable than other possible inferences that you could make about the situation you are about to face.

As I discussed earlier in this chapter, when we feel anxious it is usually about something that we consider (or infer) to be a threat to us in some way. This threat should be placed at A in the ABC framework. Since perceptions of threat, whether they are 'realistic' or not, are inferential in nature given that they are largely about future events, I distinguish between situations and perceptions of threat. I consider a situation as an accurate description of the context in which an ABC occurs. Using Brian's example, we have:

Situation: 'Being told that I will have to make a presentation in front of my peers and my boss in a week's time'

A (Threat): 'There is a good chance that I will not come across well to my peers and to my boss in this presentation'

B (Specific belief): 'I must come across well to my peers and to my boss in this presentation and I am an inadequate person if I don't'

C (Emotional consequence of **A×B**): Anxiety

You will see from the above ABC framework that anxiety is placed at C. Brian's feelings of anxiety are, in fact, the emotional consequence of his belief about the threat that he infers he will face (A×B). As we will see, there are other consequences at C about A×B and I will discuss these presently. But first, let me make a number of important observations about the ABC that I have presented.

1 *Situations don't make you anxious*

Many people think that situations make them (unhealthily) anxious. As the ABC model makes perfectly clear, this is not the case. Situations provide the context for anxiety. They do not cause anxiety. If this were the case, then we would all have to be anxious faced with the same situation. Humans are far too different for this to be the case.

2 *Threat doesn't make you anxious*

A version of the 'situations make you anxious' model is the 'threat makes you anxious' model. This is more plausible but equally incorrect. If it were true that threat makes you (unhealthily) anxious then you would all have to feel anxious when faced with threat, no matter what beliefs you held about the threat. You could not be concerned (or healthily anxious) about it. Luckily, it is possible to be concerned about threat rather than (unhealthily) anxious about it and you can do this primarily by changing your general and specific anxiety-related beliefs to general and specific concern-related beliefs. I will show you how to do this in Chapters 3 and 4. If it wasn't possible to feel concerned about threat rather than anxious about it, I would not bother to write this book and counsellors and therapists all over the world would be wasting their (and their anxious clients') time.

3 *Your feelings of anxiety stem from your unhealthy beliefs about threat*

This is the most accurate of the three models that I have presented here. It shows that in order for you to feel anxious, two conditions have to be present: threat and an anxiety-related belief about threat. Threat, on its own, leads neither to unhealthy anxiety nor to healthy concern. It needs an anxiety-related belief to lead to anxiety or a concern-related belief to lead to concern. Holding a general or specific anxiety-related belief on its own does not lead to anxiety. It requires a threat to activate it and the feelings of anxiety that accompany its activation.

Thinking consequences (at C) of anxiety-related beliefs (at B)

Once one of your anxiety-related beliefs has been fully activated and you feel anxious (at C) in a situation, this belief will also affect the way you subsequently think and what you focus on. In general, these are known as thinking consequences of your anxiety-related beliefs. Let me give you an example of this process with reference to Brian's situation. Brian became anxious when he thought about not coming across well to his peers and to his boss in his forthcoming presentation, believing that he had to come across well to them and that he would be inadequate if he didn't, and this activated belief influenced Brian's subsequent thinking. Thus, he thought that his peers would laugh at him and that his boss would give him a poor report at his next appraisal. Let me put this into the ABC framework:

Situation: 'Being told that I will have to make a presentation in front of my peers and my boss in a week's time'

A (Threat): 'There is a good chance that I will not come across well to my peers and to my boss in this presentation'

B (Specific belief): 'I must come across well to my peers and to my boss in this presentation and I am an inadequate person if I don't'

C (Emotional consequence of A×B): Anxiety
(Thinking consequences of A×B):
'I will give one of the worst presentations ever given at these events'
'My peers will laugh at me'
'My boss will give me a poor report at my next appraisal'

The thinking consequences of anxiety-related beliefs are likely to be negative and distorted in two main ways:

1 They tend to elaborate and exaggerate the negative consequences of the threat at A in the ABC framework.
2 They underestimate your ability to deal productively with the threat.

The thinking consequences of anxiety-related beliefs play an important role when our feelings of anxiety escalate, as will be discussed below.

Why anxiety escalates: the role of your thinking

You may have noticed that once you have made yourself anxious, then the more you think about what you are anxious about, the more anxious you become. Why is this? Well, one explanation for this lies in your thinking. Let me illustrate with Brian's example. In the above section, I showed you how Brian's anxiety-related belief (at B) influenced

Brian's subsequent thinking at C. Now, the type of thoughts that occur at C are inferences which, as you will recall, are hunches about reality. These inferences are most often very distorted and negative in nature and laden with threat. In Brian's case these were: 'My peers will laugh at me' and 'My boss will give me a poor report at my next appraisal.'

What happens next is interesting and important if you are to understand your anxiety problem fully. Brian then focused on the inference 'My boss will give me a poor report at my next appraisal', assuming that this was a fact rather than an inference that needed to be checked against the available facts, and this then activated another of his anxiety-related beliefs. Whenever you focus on a thinking consequence (at C) of a previous anxiety-related belief, this becomes a new A. If this then activates a new specific anxiety-related belief (at B) then you will become more anxious at C and produce even more threat-filled thinking consequences at C. You then focus on one such inference which becomes another new A which activates another anxiety-related belief at B, and so on. The diagram below outlines this process for Brian:

Situation: 'Being told that I will have to make a presentation in front of my peers and my boss in a week's time'

A (Threat): 'There is a good chance that I will not come across well to my peers and to my boss in this presentation'

B (Specific belief): I must come across well to my peers and to my boss in this presentation and I am an inadequate person if I don't'

C (Emotional consequence of **A×B**): Anxiety
(Thinking consequences of **A×B**):
'I will give one of the worst presentations ever given at these events'
'Everyone will laugh at me'
'My boss will give me a very bad report at my next appraisal'

A2 (Threat): 'My boss will give me a very bad report at my next appraisal'

B2 (Belief): 'This must not happen. It will be terrible if he gives me a poor report'

C2 (Emotional consequence of **A2×B2**): Increased anxiety

(Thinking consequence of **A2×B2**): 'I'll be fired'

↓

A3 (Threat): 'I'll be fired'

B3 (Belief): 'This must not happen. It will be terrible if I am fired'

C3 (Emotional consequence of **A3×B3**): Increased anxiety
(Thinking consequence of **A3×B3**): 'I'll never work again'

So here we have a situation where Brian is told that he will make a presentation before his peers and his boss and he soon thinks that he will never work again. How quickly this happens depends on a number of factors. Basically, the greater the imminence of the threat, the more often you have run the particular 'anxiety programme' from beginning to end and the stronger your conviction in your anxiety-related belief, the quicker you will go from 'situation' to C3 (in Brian's case).

Thinking designed to ameliorate or eradicate anxiety

So far, I have discussed thinking that is an integral part of anxiety, i.e. inferences of threat and anxiety-related beliefs. However, you may also use thinking to attempt to reduce the intensity of your anxiety or to get rid of it entirely. Here is a list of the most common of these thinking strategies:

Distraction

When you try to distract yourself from your anxiety, you attempt to focus your attention away from the threat. For example, when Brian is anxious about not coming across well to his peers and to his boss he tries to think about something else, often something pleasurable. Distraction thinking usually only brings short-term relief, if it works at all, because it doesn't help the person to challenge the anxiety-related beliefs that are at the core of their anxiety.

Reassurance thinking

When you feel anxious and you are on your own, you may attempt to reassure yourself that the threat you think you are facing won't actually happen or if it does it won't be as bad as you may think. Using this strategy, Brian would try to convince himself that there was little chance that he would not come across well to his peers and to his boss, or that if he did they might not notice it, or if they did they might make allowance for his poor performance. The problem with reassurance thinking is that because your anxiety-related belief is activated you will not be able to reassure yourself that either the threat will not happen or it won't be as bad as you think it might be. Your activated anxiety-related belief means that you are not reassurable for more than a short period of time.

Compensatory thinking

When you are anxious and you engage in compensatory thinking, you try to convince yourself that the very opposite of what you fear may happen. Thus, were Brian to engage in compensatory thinking for his anxiety about not coming across well to his peers and to his boss, he would think that his performance would be excellent and that he would make a favourable impression on his peers and his boss. He may think these things or see them happening in his mind's eye. As I will discuss throughout this book, mental images play as important a role in anxiety and its maintenance as do words, although this does vary from person to person. The trouble with compensatory thinking is that, once again, you will not be convinced by your compensatory thinking for long, given the activation of your anxiety-related belief, and it will also prevent you from identifying, challenging and changing this belief which, as I will show you later, is the core of overcoming anxiety in the longer term.

Defensive thinking

The final type of thinking that you may use to cope with your anxiety is known as defensive thinking. One of the main goals of defensive thinking is to help you diminish in your mind the importance of the threat. If you can convince yourself that the threat is not, in fact, really a threat by diminishing its importance, you will not be anxious. You can do this in a number of ways. For example, if Brian used defensive thinking he could try to tell himself that the presentation was not an important one, that it did not matter if he failed to impress his peers and his boss or that he didn't really care about his job because he could always get another one. Basically, defensive thinking involves you in an attempt to deceive yourself that what in fact is very important to you has little or no importance to you. As you can imagine, self-deception is not a good long-term solution to anxiety problems.

Some people consider reassurance thinking and defensive thinking the same, but there is a major difference between the two types of thinking and it is this: in reassurance thinking you do not attempt to diminish the importance of the threat, which is your main aim in defensive thinking.

Before leaving this issue of unhelpful thinking methods to cope with anxiety, I want to make two points. First, you can use these techniques once you have made yourself anxious or you can do so as soon as you realize that you may be facing a threat about which you would make yourself anxious if you gave yourself the chance. Second, you can be aware that you are using these methods or you may use them outside of your awareness. If the latter is the case, then fortunately you can learn to recognize that you are using them. This is important if you are to learn to overcome your anxiety effectively in the longer term.

Anxiety, behaviour and the environment

In this final section, I will discuss the role of behaviour in the development and maintenance of anxiety. Since we do not behave in a physical and social vacuum, I will also discuss how environmental responses to the way we act may also help to perpetuate our anxiety.

When you make yourself anxious about a threat because you hold an anxiety-related belief about that threat, you may act in a number of ways. Before I discuss these behaviours, I want to make the point that in the ABC framework, behaviour is placed under C. The full ABC framework is thus:

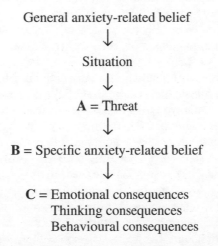

General anxiety-related belief
↓
Situation
↓
A = Threat
↓
B = Specific anxiety-related belief
↓
C = Emotional consequences
Thinking consequences
Behavioural consequences

Before I discuss anxiety-related behaviours, I want to make the same point that I made about anxiety-related thinking. You may act in ways to cope with your anxiety once you have begun to feel it and you also

29

may act so that you do not experience anxiety. In the latter case, you are aware either consciously or unconsciously that you are about to face a threat and you act in a way to remove the threat, thus warding off feelings of anxiety.

Avoidance

A very common behaviour that people engage in to deal with their anxiety is avoidance – more specifically, avoidance of situations in which you are likely, in your mind, to encounter threat. However, in trying to deal with your anxiety by avoiding threat, you are in fact deepening your anxiety problem by reinforcing your anxiety-related belief. For example, let's imagine that Brian decided to avoid the meeting where he was supposed to make his presentation. This might help him to avoid feeling anxious in the short term, but it will strengthen his general and specific anxiety-related beliefs. It is as if Brian is reasoning thus: 'Since I must come across well to my peers and to my boss and there is a chance that I might not do so, I will therefore not give the presentation.' In this way, avoidance tends to make you feel better in the short term, but leads you to get worse in the longer term.

Withdrawal

Imagine that you are in a situation and you begin to feel anxious: what would your first reaction be? The chances are it would be to withdraw from the situation. Why? Because taking flight from threat is one of our basic responses as humans, and probably had evolutionary value when our ancestors were in caves and their environment was full of dangerous animals that would pose a very real threat to their existence. Under these circumstances, taking flight helped to protect the lives of our ancestors. While we will still take flight from real danger, we are also very prone to withdraw from threats that are not life-threatening. This is particularly the case when the threat that you are anxious about has not yet materialized, or not fully so. Let me illustrate this with reference to Brian's case. If Brian does not turn up for the meeting he is in avoidant mode, but if he attends the presentation and leaves the room before the threat materializes then he is in withdrawal mode. Brian might leave the situation before his turn to talk or he might leave during his talk at the first sign that he may not be coming across well to his peers and to his boss.

Like avoidance, withdrawal helps you deal with anxiety in the short term, but not in the longer term. Withdrawal is problematic for two reasons. First, it is behaviour that is based on your anxiety-related belief and thus reinforces it. When Brian withdraws from the presentation before his turn to speak, he does so because he believes that he must come across well to his peers and to his boss and he doubts whether he will do so. His withdrawal behaviour thus strengthens his conviction in his anxiety-related belief. Second, by leaving the situation before giving his talk, Brian does not test his inference that there is a good chance he will not come across well to those present. According to the REBT model of anxiety, the first of these reasons is more serious than the second, for Brian could stay, give his talk, realize that he was wrong in thinking that it was likely that he would not come across well to his peers and to his boss, and still hold on to his anxiety-related belief that he must come across well to them. Thus, in many instances (but not all), staying in situations in which you think you may encounter threat is important because it gives you an opportunity to challenge and change your anxiety-related belief.

Safety-seeking behaviour

When you engage in safety-seeking behaviour, you tend to stay in situations in which you think you will encounter a threat, but you engage in behaviour that is designed to keep you safe from that threat. Imagine that you are anxious about going shopping in a supermarket because you might faint, a threat about which you hold a specific awfulizing belief (e.g. 'It would be awful if I fainted while going around the supermarket'). You could avoid the situation altogether (avoidance) or leave the supermarket at the first sign of faintness (withdrawal), but you decide to stay. But, because you hold the aforementioned specific anxiety-related belief, you are anxious and think that there is a very good chance that you will faint. How would you tend to deal with this situation? You would probably look for ways that would, in your mind, keep you safe from the threat. This would probably involve taking steps so that you would not faint. Thus, you might grip the shopping trolley that you are using very tightly so that you would not fall over, or you might only go shopping with a friend or relative and hold on to them as you walk up and down the aisles, again with the purpose of stopping you from fainting.

Safety-seeking behaviours are like avoidance and withdrawal in that they help you to deal with anxiety in the short term by in some way nullifying the threat that you think you would face if you did not take these steps, but they do not help you to overcome anxiety in the longer term. Indeed, they tend to maintain your anxiety. By gripping the shopping trolley or holding on to another person for dear life, you do not get the experience of challenging and changing your anxiety-related belief that it would be awful if you were to faint, nor do you get the experience of walking around the supermarket unaided and not fainting. REBT theory holds, as a matter of fact, that you are more likely to experience the latter if you have some experience of the former.

The development of safety-seeking behaviours can be quite individualistic and a large variety of actions may serve as safety-seeking behaviours, so large that an exhaustive list is not possible in a short book such as this. However, I will give a number of examples to show how broad such behaviours can be.

Superstitious behaviour

Superstitious behaviour is behaviour that, in the person's mind, wards off threat, even though it does not have the actual power to do so.

1 Mary takes half a valium tablet with her when she goes out to social events. She says that having it in her bag helps her to keep calm.
2 Whenever Bob thinks that somebody might criticize him (a threat about which he is anxious), he strokes a rabbit's foot which he keeps in his pocket. He thinks that doing so helps to prevent people criticizing him.

Obsessive–compulsive behaviour

Obsessive–compulsive behaviour is repetitive behaviour that, in the person's mind, wards off threat and keeps him or her safe.

1 Fiona wouldn't leave the house until she had checked seven times that the cooker was off. If she didn't do this, she claimed she became anxious that the cooker would blow up and destroy the house.
2 When Michael walked along a paved road, he was compelled to walk between the cracks. He considered that if he walked on the cracks then something very bad would happen to his family.

Avoidance in situ

Earlier in this section, I discussed the role that avoidance plays in anxiety, and showed that avoidance involves physical avoidance of a situation deemed by the person as threatening. Avoidance in situ, however, describes behaviour that the person undertakes to avoid the threat while remaining in the situation in which the threat is deemed to be imminent.

32

1 Mary is anxious about talking in small groups. For several weeks she stayed silent in her weekly seminar group at college, until her tutor told her that it was important for her to speak up. When she did so, she avoided looking at everyone so that she didn't see the disapproval on their faces, which was the threat that she was anxious about and sought to avoid. Both Mary's silence and her refusal to look at her fellow students while talking are examples of avoidance in situ.

2 Roger is anxious about travelling on the underground because he fears having certain thoughts on the train which he considers to be evidence that he is losing control, and he holds an anxiety-related belief about loss of control over his thoughts. Roger still travels on the underground, so he does not physically avoid his threat. However, he attempts to avoid his threat in situ mentally by listening to very loud music on his Walkman and by digging his nails into his wrist. Note that Roger tries to avoid his threat in the situation in which he predicts it happening by distracting himself from the threat.

Threat is experienced through the senses, and thus strategies destined to avoid threat in situ are in effect strategies that help you to avoid sensory experience (in Mary's case the sight of people disapproving of her and in Roger's case his own thoughts). Other people might attempt to avoid certain sounds or smells, and a very common category of threat that people strive to avoid in situ concerns a whole range of bodily sensations which are considered threats because they herald in the person's mind loss of control. Loss of control is a very common theme in anxiety.

Avoidance in situ is as effective as physical avoidance in helping you to deal with anxiety: i.e. it helps you only in the short term because it neither gives you an opportunity to challenge and change your anxiety-related beliefs nor does it enable you to see that you are overestimating the chances of the threat materializing or the negativity of the threat if it does occur.

Compensatory behaviour

The purpose of compensatory behaviour in dealing with anxiety is the same as the purpose of compensatory thinking (see p. 28). The difference is that in compensatory behaviour you put your compensatory thoughts into actual practice. If Brian were to engage in compensatory behaviour to deal with his anxiety about not coming across well to his peers and to his boss, he would overprepare his performance so that there was no chance of him doing other than brilliantly. He would try and ensure that it was the best presentation that those present had ever seen. This is the very opposite of what he fears may happen. The trouble with compensatory behaviour is that you spend all your time acting in a way to ensure that what you will fear (i.e. the threat) will not happen, so that you do not spend any time identifying, challenging and changing the anxiety-related belief that you hold about the threat that underpins your anxiety.

As I will discuss later in the book, the best long-term way of overcoming anxiety is to change your anxiety-related beliefs rather than trying to guarantee that threats to what you consider important in your personal domain will not occur.

Impulsive behaviour

When you hold anxiety-related beliefs and you think that a threat to your personal domain is imminent, then you may well act very quickly to get rid of the threat. Such impulsive behaviour is likely to make matters worse because it is based on an absence of considered, reflective thinking. Unconsidered, unreflective thinking is characteristic of anxiety.

Gerald, a lecturer, received an anonymous complaint written by one of his students and was asked by his head of department to write a reply. Instead of giving the matter due consideration and involving his union, he dashed off a reply quickly because he was anxious about the matter and believed that he had to get it off his desk and out of his mind immediately. In doing so, he made a number of errors which made matters worse for him.

Reassurance-seeking behaviour

Earlier in this chapter, I discussed how you might attempt to deal with your anxiety by attempting to reassure yourself that the threat you anticipate will not actually occur. You can also attempt to gain reassurance from others that the threat will not occur.

1 Daphne suffered from hypochondriasis and thought that small changes in her skin were signs that she was suffering from deadly skin cancer. For Daphne the threat was a new blemish and not knowing for sure that the blemish was benign. Daphne attempted to

cope with this threat by showing the blemish to friends and eliciting reassurance from them that the blemish looked harmless. She would also go to her doctor and elicit similar reassurance.

2 Peter suffered from unhealthy jealousy. As I discussed in my book *Overcoming Jealousy* (Sheldon Press, 1998), unhealthy jealousy is a complex state comprising several emotions experienced at different times. One of these emotions is anxiety. Peter often became anxious when watching television with his wife, Stephanie, particularly when he saw an attractive man on the TV screen. This posed a threat for Peter because he thought that Stephanie found this man attractive. In order to deal with this threat, Peter asked Stephanie if she found the man attractive. This reassurance-seeking behaviour always had the desired effect because Stephanie always reassured Peter that she didn't find the man attractive.

The basic aim of reassurance-seeking behaviour is to elicit reassurance from the other person that you are not in fact facing a threat. Thus, when Daphne asks her friend to look at the blemish on her arm and her friend says that she thinks it is a freckle, for a while Daphne is reassured that she is not suffering from skin cancer. Her friend's response relieves Daphne, temporarily, of the uncertainty that she finds threatening and that leads her so easily to think she has skin cancer. And when Peter asks Stephanie if she finds the man on the TV screen attractive, his aim is to elicit reassurance from her that she is not attracted to the man. When she gives it, Stephanie removes the threat for Peter, albeit temporarily.

There is nothing intrinsically wrong with reassurance, and if you are reassurable then it can be quite helpful. However, if your anxiety problem is chronic, like Daphne's and Peter's, it is likely that you have asked for reassurance about the same type of threat over and over again. If so, the relief that you derive from such reassurance is short-lived because you are not reassurable. When this happens, reassurance-seeking becomes part of the problem rather than part of the solution. This last point also applies to the other types of anxiety-related behaviour discussed in this section.

There are two aspects of reassurance-seeking behaviour that are potentially problematic: the seeking of reassurance and the giving of reassurance. Let me focus for a moment on the giving of reassurance. Whether the other person gives reassurance or withholds reassurance is important in the long-term prognosis for your anxiety problem. If it is given, it briefly relieves your anxiety by removing the threat temporarily, but makes it more likely that you will seek reassurance the next time you think you are under threat and less likely that you will identify, challenge and change the anxiety-related beliefs that underpin your anxiety problem. If the reassurance is withheld, one of two things will happen. Either you will use the opportunity to identify, challenge and change the anxiety-related belief that underpins your anxiety (assuming that you understand the role that such beliefs play in anxiety) or you will be forced to use some other palliative, short-term way of dealing with your anxious feelings.

This analysis shows that the response that you get from your environment (interpersonal and physical) to your behavioural attempts to deal with your anxiety influences whether you will overcome your anxiety problem or whether you will continue to have the problem.

This ends my analysis of anxiety. To recap, I outlined the major symptoms of anxiety and pointed out that we are largely anxious about what we perceive to be threats to important aspects of our personal domain (both ego and non-ego). I then went on to consider the central role that general and specific anxiety-related beliefs play in anxiety, and in doing so I discussed the four major forms that our anxiety-related beliefs take (demanding beliefs, awfulizing beliefs, low frustration tolerance beliefs and depreciation beliefs) before outlining the emotional, thinking and behavioural consequences of these beliefs. In this latter outline, I considered how we use thinking and behaviour to deal with anxious feelings once we have begun to experience them, or to stop us feeling them in the first place when we think that we are about to encounter a threat. I pointed out that these thinking and behavioural strategies only work in the short term and tend to get in the way of us overcoming our anxiety problems in the longer term.

In the next chapter, I will consider the nature of concern, the healthy alternative to anxiety.

2

The Nature of Concern

In this chapter, I will discuss the main components of concern, the healthy alternative to anxiety when you are facing a threat. Once again, although these components interact with one another, I will consider them one at a time. But first let me give you a general overview of these components. When you feel concern, you are less aware of your symptoms than when you feel anxious, because in concern you are focused on the threat in a constructive way whereas in anxiety your focus is not constructive and whenever your focus is unconstructive you are likely to be aware of your symptoms. Other than your symptoms, several other factors come into play when you are anxious. Thus, you bring to situations in which you feel concerned a pre-formed, general concern-related belief. You consider (or make an inference) that you are facing or are about to face some kind of threat (and when you are concerned this inference is likely to be realistic). You hold a specific belief about this threat that is usually a concrete form of the general concern-related belief that you brought to this situation. As with anxiety, this specific concern-related belief has an important impact on your subsequent thinking (including what you pay attention to) and on the way that you behave, and, in turn, your behaviour has consequences.

Let me now deal with these components one at a time.

The symptoms of concern

When you feel concern, your symptoms are similar to when you feel anxious, but there are a number of differences. First, when you feel very concerned in the face of a serious threat, your symptoms can be strong, but they tend not to be as intense as they would be if you were to be very anxious in the face of the same threat. Second, when you feel concerned your symptoms do not interfere with your sense of being in control and do not stop you from dealing with the threat in a constructive way, whereas when you are anxious your symptoms are such that you have a sense of being out of control and your attempts to deal constructively with the threat are hampered.

General concern-related beliefs

As I pointed out in Chapter 1, you are not a blank screen when you face a specific situation. Rather, you bring one or more general beliefs to a situation and these beliefs have a marked influence on whether you are likely to feel unhealthily anxious, healthily concerned or indifferent in the situation. In this section, I will concentrate on general beliefs that tend to underpin concern.

How can you recognize a concern-related belief that is general in nature? You can do so by understanding that it has two main components. First, as with a general anxiety-related belief, it has a theme that is likely to span a number of situations (e.g. being in control over your feelings, gaining approval from significant others, doing well at important tasks, being certain that a health-related symptom is benign). Second, the nature of the belief is that it is flexible and non-extreme. Since flexible and non-extreme (general and specific beliefs) are at the very core of concern, I will discuss them at some length.

General concern-related beliefs are flexible and non-extreme

The theory of Rational Emotive Behaviour Therapy (REBT) states that flexible and non-extreme beliefs, which are at the core of concern, are known as rational beliefs, but I will refer to them in this book as healthy beliefs. There are four healthy beliefs that REBT particularly highlights when considering concern. The first, and some REBT therapists such as Albert Ellis would say the most important, is flexible and is known as a *full preference belief*. A full preference belief has two components: it asserts your preference (e.g. 'I want . . .', 'I prefer . . .') and it negates your demand (e.g. '. . . but it isn't essential that I get what I want'). The other three are non-extreme and are known as *anti-awfulizing beliefs* (e.g. 'It is bad that . . . but not awful'), *high frustration tolerance (HFT) beliefs* (e.g. 'It is hard to bear when . . . but I can bear it') and *acceptance beliefs* (e.g. 'I am a fallible human being if . . .', 'You are a fallible human being if . . .' or 'The world is a complex place where good and bad things happen if . . .'). Let us take a closer look at these four healthy beliefs and see how they underpin concern. In doing so, I will return to the case of Brian, who I introduced in Chapter 1, and consider what would happen if his general beliefs were healthy rather than unhealthy.

Full preference beliefs

Let's suppose that Brian regularly felt concern (or healthy anxiety) before giving presentations at work instead of unhealthy anxiety. His general concern-related belief would contain a full preference belief as follows: 'I want to come across well to my peers and to my boss, but I don't absolutely have to do so.' As you can see, this belief contains both a theme, 'coming across well to my peers and to my boss' and a flexible, full preference belief about this theme, 'I want to ... but I don't absolutely have to do so...' In contrast to demanding beliefs, which are false, illogical and have disturbed consequences (see Chapter 1, pp. 4–6), full preference beliefs are true, logical and, perhaps most importantly, they have healthy consequences.

Why are full preference beliefs true? Well, when you genuinely hold a full preference belief about yourself, others and/or life conditions, you indicate that you want yourself, others and life conditions to be a certain way, but do not demand that your desire must be met. Both aspects of a full preference belief are true. First, it is true that you hold a particular desire and second, it is true that there is no reason why your desire has to be met. Brian's full preference belief is true, because he can prove that he wants to come across well to his peers and to his boss and he can also prove that there is no law of nature which decrees that he must do so.

Why are full preference beliefs logical? a full preference belief is logical because it contains two parts which are flexible (i.e. 'I want ...' and '... but I don't have to get what I want') and the second part logically follows from the first. Thus, Brian's flexible full preference belief can for our purposes be expressed thus: 'I want to come across well to my peers and to my boss [flexible], but there is no law of nature which decrees that I must do so [flexible].' As philosophers will tell you, a flexibility can logically follow from another related flexibility. Thus, full preference beliefs are logical because they contain two flexible parts logically linked together.

Finally, why are full preference beliefs largely constructive? Because they very frequently lead to feelings of concern, realistic thinking and constructive behaviour. When Brian prefers to come over well to his peers and to his boss, but does not demand that he does so and acknowledges to himself that his preference might not be met, then he is concerned but not anxious about this eventuality, because his belief allows him to accept the possibility of him not coming across well. When Brian holds a full preference belief, but

39

not a demanding one, this is an outcome that he prefers not to happen without him demanding that it must not occur. While anxiety is frequently the result when there is a conflict between what is (or may be) and what must be when these are radically different and when you think that what may be is likely to happen (as discussed in Chapter 1), concern is frequently the result when there is a conflict between what is (or may be) and what you prefer but do not demand, again when these are radically different and when you think that what may be is again likely to occur. Thus, for Brian, what may be is that he may fail to come across well to his peers and to his boss, whereas what he prefers but does not demand is to come across well to them.

In addition, full preference beliefs frequently lead to realistic thinking and problem-solving-based behaviour. Thus, when Brian sees that he may not come across well to his peers and to his boss and holds the belief that he wants to come across well to them, while at the same time accepting that he doesn't have to do so, then he is likely to engage in realistic, balanced thinking like 'Some may hate what I have to say, but others will like it and yet others will think that it's OK', 'Some people may think that I'm an idiot if I don't come across well, but most won't think that I am' and 'If I don't come over well, it may affect my bonus at the end of the year, but there are many other factors that will be taken into consideration when my bonus is calculated.' These thoughts reflect the flexibility and balance that are the hallmarks of full preference beliefs (see p. 5 for thoughts that stem from Brian's demanding belief and compare those with the above thoughts).

Full preference beliefs also frequently lead to constructive behaviour. Thus, when Brian sees that he may not come across well to his peers and to his boss and holds the belief that he would prefer to come across well to them, without insisting that he must do so, then he is likely to focus on what he is saying rather than how he is saying it. Consequently, he is likely to speak fluently, at a pace which allows his audience to digest what he is saying, and he is likely to engage his audience in appropriate eye contact. He would certainly not contemplate feigning illness and cancelling his presentation, which he might do if he was anxious (see pp. 5–6 for a discussion of Brian's anxiety-related behaviour as a point of comparison). As you can see, then, full preference beliefs can have a useful effect on a person's psychological state and functioning.

Anti-awfulizing beliefs

As we have seen, Brian regularly became concerned before giving presentations at work. His general concern-related belief also contained an anti-awfulizing belief, as follows: 'It would be bad if I did not come across well to my peers and to my boss, but it wouldn't be awful.' As you can see, this belief contains both a theme, 'not coming across well to my peers and to my boss', and a non-extreme anti-awfulizing belief about this theme, 'It would be bad, but not awful if . . .' As I showed in Chapter 1, awfulizing beliefs are false, illogical and have disturbed consequences, whereas anti-awfulizing beliefs are true, logical and have healthy consequences.

Anti-awfulizing beliefs are true for three reasons. First, they are true because they imply that even if the threat materializes, things can still get worse. If Brian does not come across well to his peers and to his boss, his anti-awfulizing belief helps him to see that many things can be worse than this. Second, anti-awfulizing beliefs are true because they imply that events can be placed along a continuum of badness from 0 to 99.99 per cent, whereas the term 'awful' implies that things can be worse than 100 per cent bad. In holding to his anti-awfulizing belief, Brian can prove that not coming across well to his peers and to his boss can be placed along the badness continuum. The third reason why anti-awfulizing beliefs are true is that they imply that good can come from bad. Thus, his anti-awfulizing belief would help Brian acknowledge that if he did not come across well to his peers and to his boss, he could still learn from this situation and improve his presentation skills.

Why are anti-awfulizing beliefs logical? An anti-awfulizing belief is logical because it contains two parts which are non-extreme (i.e. 'it is bad . . .' and '. . . but it isn't terrible') and the second part logically follows from the first. Thus, Brian's non-extreme anti-awfulizing belief can for our purposes be expressed thus: 'It is bad if I don't come across well to my peers and to my boss [non-extreme], but it isn't terrible [non-extreme].' As philosophers will tell you, something that is not extreme can logically follow from another related non-extremity. Thus, anti-awfulizing beliefs are logical because they contain two non-extreme parts logically linked together.

Finally, why are anti-awfulizing beliefs largely constructive? For the same reason that full preference beliefs are predominantly constructive. Because they very frequently lead to feelings of concern, realistic thinking and constructive behaviour. When Brian holds that it would be bad but not awful if he does not come over well to his peers and to his boss and he acknowledges to himself that this might happen, then he is concerned about this eventuality because he is giving it a non-extreme negative evaluation. Concern is frequently the result when you think that something bad may happen and you believe that it would be bad, but not awful, terrible or the end of the world were it to happen.

Anti-awfulizing does not only lead to you experiencing feelings of concern, it also frequently leads to realistic thinking and problem-solving behaviour. Thus, when Brian sees that he may not come across well to his peers and to his boss and believes that it would be bad but not awful if this happened, then he is likely to engage in thinking which is consistent with 'badness' rather than with 'horror'. Thus, he may think that people will have a variety of responses to his presentation. While he might think that they would heckle him or leave the room in droves if he held an awfulizing belief about not coming across well to the gathered assembly, his anti-awfulizing belief would lead him to conclude that these responses would be too extreme. Rather, he might think that those who thought negatively of his presentation might talk about it briefly among themselves, and that some people might give him some suggestions about how he could come across better in future presentations.

If he held an awfulizing belief, he might think that failing to come across well to his peers and to his boss might be the end of his career and that no-one would ever employ him again (as discussed in Chapter 1). However, Brian's anti-awfulizing belief would see that these grossly exaggerated scenarios were very unlikely, and that the worst that would probably happen would be that his boss would discuss his performance with him, and, if he had given presentations before that were not very good, his boss would formally suggest remedial action to help him improve his performance in this area.

Furthermore, anti-awfulizing beliefs frequently lead to construc-tive behaviour. Thus, when Brian sees that he may not come across well to his peers and to his boss and believes that it would be bad but not awful if that happened, then he is likely to act in ways that are very similar to how he would act when he held a full preference belief about such situations (e.g. he is likely to speak fluently, at a pace which allows his audience to digest what he is saying, and he is likely to engage his audience in appropriate eye contact; he will certainly not contemplate feigning illness and cancelling his presentation). Like full preference beliefs, anti-awfulizing beliefs have a beneficial effect on a person's psychological state and functioning.

High frustration tolerance (HFT) beliefs

By now, you will know that Brian regularly feels concerned but not anxious before giving presentations at work. His general concern-related belief also contains a high frustration tolerance (HFT) belief as follows: 'It would be difficult for me to bear not coming across well to my peers and to my boss, but I could tolerate it and it would be worth tolerating.' As you can see, this belief contains both a theme, 'not coming across well to my peers and to my boss', and a non-extreme HFT belief about this theme: 'It would be difficult for me to bear . . . but I could tolerate it.' Unlike LFT beliefs which are false, illogical and have largely disturbed consequences, HFT beliefs are true, logical and have healthy consequences.

Why are HFT beliefs true? Because they correspond to reality. Brian can prove that not coming across well to his peers and to his boss is difficult to bear and he can also prove that he can tolerate it. After all, he is not likely to disintegrate and die, nor will he lose the capacity to experience happiness in the future if he fails to come across well to the gathered assembly. Since Brian sees that it is in his interests to tolerate the possibility of not coming across well to his peers and to his boss, he decides to risk this possibility.

Why are HFT beliefs logical? An HFT belief is logical because it contains two parts which are non-extreme (i.e. 'it is difficult to bear . . .' and '. . . but it is bearable') and the second part logically follows from the first. Thus, Brian's non-extreme HFT belief can for our purposes be expressed thus: 'It will be difficult to bear if I don't come across well to my peers and to my boss [non-extreme], but it is bearable [non-extreme] and it is worth bearing.' As I mentioned above, something that is not extreme can logically follow from another related non-extremity. Thus, HFT beliefs are logical because they contain two non-extreme parts logically linked together.

Finally, why are HFT beliefs largely constructive? Because, like full preference and anti-awfulizing beliefs, they lead to feelings of concern, realistic thinking and constructive behaviour. Thus, when Brian holds that it would be difficult to bear but bearable if he did not come over well to his peers and to his boss and he acknowledges to himself that this might happen, then he feels concerned about this eventuality because he sees this situation as posing a challenge to his perceived ability to tolerate such situations.

As I said above, holding HFT beliefs also leads to realistic thinking. Thus, when Brian sees that he may not come across well to his peers and to his boss and believes that he would be able to bear it if this happened, although he would find this difficult, then he is likely to engage in thinking which is consistent with his perceived ability to tolerate the event. Thus, he may think that he would lose some control of himself if he remained in the situation, but would still be largely in control. For example, he may predict that he would feel concerned and that some of those present might detect this. Compare this thinking with his thinking based on his LFT belief: 'I will lose complete control and everyone at the presentation will see this.'

As already noted, HFT beliefs frequently lead to constructive behaviour. Thus, when Brian sees that he may not come across well to his peers and to his boss and believes that he would be able to bear it if this happened, although it would be difficult but worth doing, then he is likely to act in ways that are very similar to how he would act when he held a full preference belief or an anti-awfulizing belief in such situations. Thus, he would prepare thoroughly for the presentation without going over the top (as opposed to trying to get out of it or overpreparing for it), and during the presentation he would speak fluently at an appropriate pace and with appropriate eye contact with his audience (as opposed to stumbling over his words, speaking too quickly or avoiding engaging in appropriate eye contact with his peers and with his boss). Like full preference beliefs and anti-awfulizing beliefs, HFT beliefs have a largely constructive effect on a person's psychological state and functioning.

Acceptance beliefs

In Chapter 1, I pointed out that there are two major types of (unhealthy) anxiety: ego anxiety and non-ego anxiety. Similarly, there are two types of concern: ego concern and non-ego concern. Both types of concern are based on all four healthy beliefs outlined on p. 38 (i.e. full preference beliefs, anti-awfulizing beliefs, HFT beliefs and acceptance beliefs). Where they differ is with respect to the kind of acceptance beliefs being held. When your feelings of concern are ego based then your acceptance beliefs are about yourself; I will call these beliefs self-acceptance beliefs throughout this book. However, when your concern is non-ego based, then your acceptance beliefs are about others or about the world or life conditions. In this section, I will consider acceptance beliefs with reference to self-acceptance beliefs, but what I have to say also applies to acceptance beliefs about others and about the world/life conditions.

Let us now return to Brian who, for our purposes here, experienced concern before giving presentations at work. His general concern-related belief contained a self-acceptance belief as follows: 'If I do not come across well to my peers and to my boss, this will not prove that I am an inadequate person. Rather, I am a fallible human being with a complex mixture of strengths and weaknesses.' As you can see, this belief contains both a theme, 'not coming across well to my peers and to my boss', and a non-extreme belief about Brian in relation to this theme, 'I am not an inadequate person, I am a fallible human being . . .' As with full preference beliefs, anti-awfulizing beliefs and HFT beliefs, self-acceptance beliefs are true, logical and have healthy consequences.

Why are self-acceptance beliefs true? Well, when you accept yourself, you are saying, in effect, that your entire 'self' is too complex to merit a single rating. You can prove this and, furthermore, you can prove that you are a fallible human being and that you have adequacies and inadequacies. For a detailed discussion of self-acceptance see my book on the subject entitled *How to Accept Yourself* (Sheldon Press, 1999).

Why are self-acceptance beliefs logical? Essentially, because you refrain from making the part–whole error. When Brian accepts himself for not coming across well to his peers and to his boss, he is saying that his 'self' [whole] cannot be defined by him not coming across well to his peers and to his boss [part]. He does acknowledge that his 'self' incorporates this part, but cannot logically be defined by it.

Finally, why are self-acceptance beliefs largely constructive? Yes, you've guessed it – because they very frequently lead to feelings of concern, realistic thinking and constructive behaviour. When Brian acknowledges to himself that he might not come over well to his peers and his boss but accepts himself if this happens, then he will make himself concerned (but not anxious) about events where this may happen. His subsequent thinking is likely to be realistic and focus on his strengths as well as his weaknesses (internal ego focus). His view of others' opinions of him (external focus) is likely to be balanced. If his presentation was average then he would acknowledge that some might view his performance negatively, but that others wouldn't. If his performance was poor he would acknowledge that some might think negatively of him as a person, but that others wouldn't overgeneralize. With respect to his behaviour, Brian's self-acceptance belief would help him to do well during his presentation as already discussed (e.g. he would speak clearly and slowly, and engage in appropriate eye contact). Once again, self-acceptance can have a useful effect on a person's psychological state.

Threat: what you feel concerned about

In Chapter 1, you will recall that I said you tend to feel (unhealthily) anxious about events that you consider to be threatening to you in some way. I also pointed out in that chapter that threat on its own does not cause you to feel anxious. Rather, you need to hold an anxiety-related belief (general or specific) about that threat in order to feel anxious, as shown in the diagram below:

Threat + anxiety-related belief = anxiety

Interestingly enough, when you feel concerned, it is also about events that you consider to be threatening (as is the case with anxiety). But the reason that you feel concerned rather than anxious about a threat is because you hold a concern-related belief (rather than an anxiety-related belief) about it, as can be seen below:

Threat + concern-related belief = concern

The impact of beliefs on threat-related inferences

In Chapter 1, I showed the effect that holding general anxiety-related beliefs has on what the person finds threatening. As can be seen in the diagram below, Brian's general anxiety-related belief leads him to focus on threatening aspects of a specific situation of being told that he had to give a presentation the following week. Note that the nature of the threat is consistent with the content of his general anxiety-related belief:

Brian's general anxiety-related belief	→ Specific event	→ Threat
I must come across well to my peers and to my boss and I am an inadequate person if I don't.	News of forthcoming presentation to peers and to boss where I may not come across well.	There is a good chance that I will not come across well.

46

Now let's see what happens if Brian holds a general concern-related belief:

Brian's general concern-related belief	→*Specific event*	→*Inference*
I want to come across well to my peers and to my boss, but I don't have to do so. If I don't, I am not inadequate. Rather, I am a fallible human being who has strengths and weaknesses.	News of forthcoming presentation to peers and to boss where I may not come across well.	If I prepare well, there is a good chance that I'll do well.

When Brian's general belief is concern-related rather than anxiety-related, he does not perceive being told that he has to give the presentation as threatening. His first thought (or inference) is realistic (that if he prepares well, there is a good chance that he will do well). In other words, he does not see threat where objectively none yet exists.

Let me reiterate the different effects that holding general anxiety-related beliefs and holding concern-related beliefs have on what you find threatening:

1 We bring our general anxiety-related beliefs (e.g. Brian's belief: 'I must come across well to my peers and to my boss and I am an inadequate person if I don't') to situations. When we encounter a specific situation where the content of the general belief *may* become reality (e.g. when Brian learns about the forthcoming presentation where he may not come across well), this belief leads us to focus on the relevant threatening aspects of the situation (e.g. Brian focuses on the possibility of not coming across well rather than on coming across well or on what he is going to say).

2 We bring our general concern-related beliefs (e.g. Brian's belief: 'I want to come across well to my peers, but I don't have to do so. If I don't, I am not an inadequate person, but a fallible human being with strengths and weaknesses') to situations. When we encounter a specific situation where the content of the general belief *may* become reality (e.g. when Brian learns about the forthcoming presentation where he may not come across well), this belief leads us to focus on the realistic aspects of the situation

(e.g. Brian focuses on the possibility of coming across well if he prepares well). Threat is not inferred unless threat realistically exists.

But when does holding a general concern-related belief lead you to infer the existence of threat? The answer is when that threat objectively exists (e.g. where neutral observers agree on the existence of that threat). For example, the diagram below outlines the circumstances under which Brian (holding a general concern-related belief) would infer the existence of threat.

Brian's general concern-related → *Specific event* → *Threat*
belief

I want to come across well to my peers and to my boss, but I don't have to do so. If I don't, I am not inadequate. Rather, I am a fallible human being who has strengths and weaknesses.	News of forthcoming presentation to peers and to boss where I may not come across well. I do not prepare.	There is a good chance that I will not come across well.

This diagram shows that when Brian does not prepare for this presentation, he infers accurately that, as a result, there is a good chance that he will not come across well to his peers and to his colleagues. This constitutes a threat to him, given his general concern-related belief.

In conclusion, bringing a general anxiety-related belief to a relevant situation means that you are more likely to focus on the threatening aspects of that situation than you would be if you brought a general concern-related belief to that situation.

Ego and non-ego threat revisited

In Chapter 1, I distinguished between two types of threat: ego and non-ego (see pp. 16–20 for a discussion of these types of threat). In doing so, I talked about the concept of the personal domain which refers to those people (including ourselves), objects and principles in which we have a personal involvement or investment. These people, objects and principles may occupy a place on the periphery of our personal domain, at a midway point within it or at the very core of it.

Generally speaking, given the presence of a concern-related belief, when something or someone towards the core of our personal domain is threatened, our feelings of concern are more intense than when someone or something occupying a less central (middle or peripheral) position within this domain is threatened.

As I showed in Chapter 1, when you hold an anxiety-related belief about a threat to the ego part of your personal domain then you will experience ego anxiety. (See p. 17 for a list of situations that constitute a threat to your ego. They are the same in concern as they are in anxiety.) Thus:

Threat to ego (or self-esteem) + anxiety-related belief = ego anxiety

Now, when you hold a concern-related belief about the same ego threat then you will experience what might be called ego concern. Thus:

Threat to ego + concern-related belief = ego concern

Similarly, when you hold an anxiety-related belief about a threat to the non-ego part of your personal domain then you will experience non-ego anxiety. (See p. 18 for a list of situations that constitute a threat to the non-ego aspects of your personal domain. They are the same in concern as they are in anxiety.) Thus:

Threat to non-ego + anxiety-related belief = non-ego anxiety

Now, when you hold a concern-related belief about the same non-ego threat then you will experience what might be called non-ego concern. Thus:

Threat to non-ego + concern-related belief = non-ego concern

Applying the important principle that I emphasized at the end of the previous section, let me stress that when you bring your general concern-related beliefs to relevant situations you will tend to infer the existence of threat when this clearly exists. This applies to both general ego and non-ego concern-related beliefs. Contrast this with what happens when you bring your general anxiety-related beliefs to the same situations.

Why not re-read the cases of Harriet (see pp. 18–19) and Sarah (see p. 19) and see if you can work out what would happen to their inferences of threat if they held a general ego concern-related belief and general non-ego concern-related belief respectively.

Specific concern-related beliefs

So far, I have discussed concern-related beliefs that are general in nature, i.e. which apply to a range of relevant situations. However, concern-related beliefs can also be specific in nature and apply to the specific situation in which you find yourself. Let me return to the case of Brian to make clear the distinction between general and specific concern-related beliefs. If you recall, the concern-related belief that Brian held which has been the focus for discussion was as follows: 'I want to come across well to my peers and to my boss, but I don't have to do so. If I do not, I am not an inadequate person. Rather, I am a fallible human being with strengths and weaknesses.' This is a general belief because it applies to all relevant situations where Brian considers that he may not come across well to these people. It encompasses the specific situation where Brian was told that he (and his group) would have to make a presentation before his peers and his boss, and it applies to other similar situations as well.

Brian's specific concern-related belief that he held about the specific situation under consideration was as follows: 'When I give my presentation next week, I want to come across well to my peers and to my boss in this situation, but I don't have to do so. If I don't, this doesn't prove that I am an inadequate person. It proves that I am a fallible human being who hasn't performed well on this occasion.' As you can see, Brian's specific concern-related belief is a concrete version of his general concern-related belief. It differs from the latter in that it specifies the situation that Brian is concerned about (i.e. the specific forthcoming occasion when Brian would have to give an actual presentation).

You will recall that Brian brings his *general* concern-related belief to the specific event and focuses on a realistic aspect of this situation (i.e. if he prepares well, he is likely to do well). This is shown in the diagram below:

General concern-related belief (GCB)
('I want to come across well to my peers and to my boss, but I
don't have to do so. If I don't, I am not an inadequate person.
Rather, I am a fallible human being with strengths and
weaknesses')
↓

Relevant specific situation
(Forthcoming presentation)
↓

Focus on realistic aspect of the situation
('There is a good chance that if I prepare well,
I will do well in my presentation')

If Brian focuses on this realistic aspect of the situation, then he will
feel neither concerned nor anxious because this realistic aspect does
not constitute a threat to him. Remember that, without threat, people
have no reason to feel anxious or concerned. But what if Brian does
not prepare well for this specific presentation? Now, we have:

General concern-related belief (GCB)
('I want to come across well to my peers and to my boss, but I
don't have to do so.' If I don't, I am not an inadequate person.
Rather, I am a fallible human being with strengths and
weaknesses')
↓

Relevant specific situation
(Forthcoming presentation without proper preparation)
↓

Focus on realistic threat
('There is a good chance that I will not come across well to my
peers and to my boss in this presentation')

This diagram shows, then, that when Brian holds a general concern-
related belief, he will perceive threat when there is good reason for
him to do so (i.e. when he has not prepared for the presentation), but
he will not do so in the absence of good cause (see previous diagram

on p. 51). Compare this to the diagram on p. 21 in Chapter 1, where Brian brings his general anxiety-related belief to the news that he has to give a forthcoming presentation. In this scenario, he focuses on a threatening aspect of the situation straight away, well before he has a good reason to do so.

Now let's see what happens when Brian makes the inference that there is a good chance that he will not come across well to his peers and to his boss, having failed to prepare properly for the presentation. Remember, in this scenario, Brian originally brought a general concern-related belief to the news that he had to give a presentation the following week. One of two possibilities will happen. First, having now focused on this threatening aspect of this specific situation, Brian now appraises this specific threat (rather than the situation itself) with the *specific* version of his concern-related belief, i.e. 'When I give *this* presentation, I want to come across well to my peers and to my boss, but I don't have to do so. If I don't, this does not prove that I am an inadequate person. Rather, it proves that I am a fallible human being who did not perform well on this occasion.' This is shown in the diagram below:

General concern-related belief (GCB)
('I want to come across well to my peers and to my boss, but I don't have to do so. If I don't, it does not prove that I am an inadequate person. Rather, it proves that I am a fallible human being with strengths and weaknesses')

Relevant specific situation
(Forthcoming presentation without proper preparation)

Focus on realistic threat
('There is a good chance that I will not come across well to my peers and to my boss in this presentation')

Specific concern-related belief
('I want to come across well to my peers and to my boss in this presentation, but I don't have to do so. If I don't, I am not an inadequate person. Rather I am a fallible human being who has not done well on this occasion')

Second, having now focused on this threatening aspect of this specific situation, Brian now appraises this specific threat (rather than the situation itself) with the specific version of his anxiety-related belief, i.e. 'When I give *this* presentation, I must come across well to my peers and to my boss, but I don't have to do so. If I don't, this proves that I am an inadequate person.') This scenario shows that you can hold a general concern-related belief which protects you from inferring threat in a specific situation when there is not a good objective reason for doing so; but when there is a good reason for inferring threat in this specific situation, then you may make yourself anxious about it because you hold a specific anxiety-related belief about this specific threat. This is shown in the diagram below:

General concern-related belief (GCB)
('I want to come across well to my peers and to my boss, but I don't have to do so. If I don't, it does not prove that I am an inadequate person. Rather, it proves that I am a fallible human being with strengths and weaknesses')

↓

Relevant specific situation
(Forthcoming presentation without proper preparation)

↓

Focus on realistic threat
('There is a good chance that I will not come across well to my peers and to my boss in this presentation')

↓

Specific anxiety-related belief
('I must come across well to my peers and to my boss in this presentation. If I don't, I am an inadequate person')

In this situation, it is as if Brian is saying: 'Generally, I don't have to come across well to my peers and to my boss, but on this occasion I do.' Having said this, let me make two points:

1 When you hold a general concern-related belief and you face a specific relevant threat, you are more likely to hold a specific concern-related belief about that threat than a specific anxiety-

related belief (although, as the above diagram shows, your specific belief can be anxiety-related).

2 When you hold a general anxiety-related belief and you face a specific relevant threat, you are much more likely to hold a specific anxiety-related belief about that threat than a specific concern-related belief. In the latter case, using Brian's example, it is as if he is saying: 'Generally, I have to come across well to my peers and to my boss, but I don't have to on this occasion.' When this happens, Brian's inference of the specific situation is that the costs of not coming across well to his peers and to his boss are not great.

Finally, let me say that while general concern-related beliefs are composed of full preference beliefs, anti-awfulizing beliefs, HFT beliefs and acceptance beliefs about general situations, specific concern-related beliefs are also composed of these beliefs, but these are held about specific situations.

Concern and thinking

In the previous chapter, I argued that thinking plays a central role in anxiety. What role does it play in concern? Let me answer this question by referring again to the ABC framework which, if you recall, in its simplest form is as follows:

$$A = \text{Activating event}$$
$$B = \text{Belief}$$
$$C = \text{Consequences}$$

Beliefs (B)

Let me again start with B, which stands for beliefs. You will recall that beliefs are fully evaluative thoughts that underpin our emotions. There are basically two types of beliefs that we may hold about events: healthy and unhealthy. In the previous chapter, I discussed the unhealthy (general and specific) beliefs which underpin anxiety, and in this chapter I have concentrated on the healthy (general and specific) beliefs that underpin concern.

Inferences of threat (at A)

As noted in the simple ABC framework, A stands for 'activating event'. You will recall from Chapter 1 that an activating event can be an actual situation (in Brian's case, being told that he had to give a presentation to his peers and to his boss in a week's time) or it can be an inference about this event. To remind you, an inference is a thought and can be best seen as a hunch about the actual situation that goes beyond the data at hand. The inference may be accurate or inaccurate, but more data are needed before the accuracy (or inaccuracy) of this inference can be determined. An example of an inference is the one Brian made about his forthcoming presentation when he failed to prepare properly for his presentation: 'There is a good chance that I will not come across well to my peers and to my boss when I give my presentation next week.' Inferences can be specific (most frequently about specific events, as in the above example) or they can be more general (about more general categories of events).

As I discussed earlier in this chapter, when you bring a general concern-related belief to a relevant situation, any inferences that you make about this situation are likely to be realistic. If there is no reason for you to infer threat then you won't, but if there is then you will. Contrast this with the scenario when you bring a general anxiety-related belief to the same relevant situation. Here, you will tend to infer threat (consistent with the content of this belief) even when none can be objectively said to exist. So when you bring a general concern-related belief to a relevant situation, your inference of threat at A in the ABC framework is realistic (see Brian's inference in the previous paragraph). If your specific belief (B) about this inferred (realistic) threat (A) is healthy, then you will feel concerned about this threat at C. Thus, concern at C stems from A×B. Using Brian's example, the following diagram summarizes the points I have made here:

General concern-related belief: 'I want to come across well to my peers and to my boss, but I don't have to do so. If I don't, I am not an inadequate person. Rather I am a fallible human being with strengths and weaknesses'

↓

Situation: Not properly preparing for the presentation

↓

A (Realistic threat): 'There is a good chance that I will not come across well to my peers and to my boss in this presentation'

B (Specific concern-related belief): 'I want to come across well to my peers and to my boss in this presentation, but I don't have to do so. If I don't then I am fallible for not doing well on this occasion, not an inadequate person'

C (Emotional consequence of **A×B**): Concern

Thinking consequences (at C) of concern-related beliefs (at B)

Once one of your concern-related beliefs has been fully activated and you feel concerned in a situation, this belief will also affect the way you subsequently think and what you focus on. These are known as thinking consequences of your concern-related beliefs. Let me give you an example of this process with reference to Brian's example. When Brian became concerned about not coming across well to his peers and to his boss because he had not properly prepared for his forthcoming presentation and because he held a healthy belief about this threat (i.e. 'I want to come across well to my peers and to my boss in this forthcoming presentation, and if I don't, it will not prove that I am an inadequate person. Rather, it will prove that I am a fallible human being who did not perform well on this occasion'), this activated belief influenced Brian's subsequent thinking. Thus, he thought that his performance would not be good, but hardly the worst ever given at such presentations. Some of his peers might laugh at him, but that most wouldn't, and that his boss would not necessarily give him a poor report at his next appraisal, unless he performed poorly in other areas in his job. Let me put these latter details into the ABC framework:

Situation: Not properly preparing for the presentation

↓

A (Realistic threat): 'There is a good chance that I will not come across well to my peers and to my boss in this presentation'

B (Specific concern-related belief): 'I want to come across well to my peers and to my boss in this presentation, but I don't have to do so. If I don't then I am fallible for not doing well on this occasion, not an inadequate person'

C (Emotional consequence of **A×B**): Concern
(Thinking consequences of **A×B**): 'My performance might not be good but it would hardly be the worst ever given at such presentations'

'Some of my peers will laugh at me, but most won't'
'My boss may give me a poor report at my next appraisal, but only if I perform poorly in other areas of my job, in addition to giving a poor presentation'

In general, the thinking consequences of concern-related beliefs tend to have two main features.

1 They tend to place the negative consequences of the threat (at A in the ABC framework) in a balanced and realistic context.
2 They demonstrate a realistic view of your ability to deal productively with the threat.

Compare these with the thinking consequences of anxiety-related beliefs (see Chapter 1, p. 25) which tend to be distorted and unrealistic. Since the thinking consequences of concern-related beliefs are generally realistic and balanced in nature they allow you to change what can be changed in the situation, and to adjust constructively if the situation can't be changed. Compare this to the threat-filled thinking consequences of anxiety-related beliefs that play such an important role in escalating anxiety (see Chapter 1, pp. 26–7).

Concern and problem-solving thinking

In the previous chapter, I showed how you use various thinking strategies to ameliorate anxiety once you have started to experience it or to avoid feeling anxiety at all. The most common of these strategies are distraction, reassurance thinking, compensatory thinking and defensive thinking, and you use these strategies mainly to avoid focusing on the threat or to transform the threat in some way so that it becomes non-threatening. I pointed out that these strategies only 'work' in the short term and do not help you to overcome your anxiety in the longer term. As I will show you in the subsequent chapters, the best way to do this is to change your unhealthy (general and specific) anxiety-related beliefs to healthy concern-related ones.

As I have shown you in this chapter, concern is underpinned by full preference beliefs, anti-awfulizing beliefs, HFT beliefs and acceptance beliefs. As such, when you hold such beliefs, you will not have to use distraction, reassurance thinking, compensatory thinking and defensive thinking, because these beliefs encourage you to acknowledge that the threat exists and encourage you to engage in problem-solving thinking to help you to change the threat if it can be changed or to adjust constructively to the threat if it can't be changed.

What is problem-solving thinking?

As the name implies, problem-solving thinking is thinking that is applied to problems and attempts to solve these problems. In the context of anxiety, it involves attempts to deal with threat if and when it materializes. There are seven stages to problem-solving thinking as applied to threat:

1 Identify the threat to be dealt with as clearly and as unambiguously as possible.
2 List all the possible ways of dealing constructively with the threat.
3 List the pros and cons of each alternative possible way of dealing constructively with the threat.
4 Choose from your list the best alternative.
5 Plan how to implement this alternative, deciding on the steps you need to take to do this. Making a written step-by-step plan at this point is particularly useful.
6 Imagine yourself implementing this step-by-step plan with the threat.
7 After you have implemented your chosen alternative with the threat, review what happened and decide what further steps you need to take to deal with the threat more effectively.

Concern, behaviour and the environment

In this final section, I will explore the relationship between concern and behaviour and discuss the effects that environmental responses to our concern-related behaviour have on our functioning.

When you feel concerned about a realistic threat because you hold a concern-related belief about that threat, you may act in a number of ways. Before I discuss these behaviours, I want to make the point that in the ABC framework behaviour is placed under C. The full ABC framework as it relates to concern is thus:

General concern-related belief

↓

Situation

↓

A = Realistic threat

↓

B = Specific concern-related belief

↓

C = Emotional consequences
Thinking consequences
Behavioural consequences

Facing the threat

A very common behaviour that people engage in when they feel concerned but not anxious about a threat is to face it rather than to avoid it (which they would do if they felt anxious about it). This is why Brian will still give his presentation even though he hasn't prepared properly for it (which constitutes a realistic threat). He is able to do this because his belief about the possibility of not coming across well to his peers and to his boss is healthy (i.e. 'I want to come across well to my peers and to my boss in this presentation, but I don't have to do so. If I don't, this proves that I am a fallible human being who hasn't done well on this occasion. It does not prove that I am inadequate').

While you will tend to face up to threat when you are concerned rather than avoid it, you are basically flexible in this respect. For example, while Brian will tend to give his presentation even though there is realistically a good chance that he won't come across well to his peers and to his boss, given that he hasn't prepared properly for his talk, there may be times when he will avoid it. For example, if he suddenly learns the night before that the head of the company is coming to the presentation and has an agenda of sacking people who come across poorly in their presentations, then he may decide to avoid this situation. The difference between anxiety-based avoidance and concern-based avoidance is that in the former you are avoiding a threat which largely exists in your mind and has no basis in reality, and in the latter you are avoiding a serious threat which is realistic and which is in your long-term interests to avoid.

In summary, concern-related beliefs lead you to face up to threat, but you may decide not to do so if it is in your best, healthy interests not to do so.

Staying in the situation

In Chapter 1, I showed that when you begin to feel anxious in a situation, your first reaction would be to withdraw from the situation. However, if instead you began to feel concerned, you would be more likely to stay in the situation and deal with the threat as best you could. This is because your concern-related belief leads you to engage in problem-solving thinking (see the previous section) and if you can give yourself thinking space in the situation such thinking will help you to act constructively. And even if you aren't able to claim such thinking space, you will still tend to stay in the situation and do the best you can because your concern-based, anti-awfulizing belief will encourage you to do so.

Staying in situations in which you think threat is imminent is important for two reasons. First, it enables you to further deepen your concern-related beliefs, and second, it gives you the opportunity to test your inference that you are, in fact, facing an imminent threat.

Resourceful behaviour

If you hold a concern-related belief, your subsequent behaviour is likely to be constructive. This belief enables you to use whatever resources you have to deal with the threat, should it materialize. As such you will tend not to act in ways that are associated with anxiety (e.g. avoidance, withdrawal, safety-seeking behaviour, impulsive behaviour, reassurance-seeking behaviour and compensatory behaviour), all of which are designed to get rid of the threat – a strategy that 'works' only in the short term and actually prevents you from overcoming your anxiety in the longer term.

Let me revisit some of the scenarios and people that I discussed in Chapter 1 (see pp. 31–5) and show how they would have acted if they held concern-related beliefs as opposed to anxiety-related beliefs. The pages at the end of each case indicate where the anxiety version can be found to aid comparison.

1 If you are concerned about going shopping in a supermarket because you might faint, a threat about which you hold a specific anti-awfulizing belief (e.g. 'It would be bad if I fainted while going around the supermarket, but it wouldn't be awful'), you would walk around it unaided and without gripping the trolley for support. This would enable you to test whether or not you would faint, and if you did, you would deal with it constructively by getting up, resting if you needed to and then finishing your shopping. (See pp. 31–5.)

2 Mary goes to social events without taking half a valium tablet with her and uses the techniques that she learned in counselling to deal with what she found threatening. (See p. 32.)

3 Whenever Bob thought that somebody might criticize him, he refrained from stroking a rabbit's foot which he kept in his pocket. Instead he practised his newly developed concern-related belief about being criticized. (See p. 32.)

4 Fiona left her house having checked once that the cooker was off. Once she left she rehearsed the concern-related belief that she didn't need to know for sure that the cooker would not blow up and destroy the house and that she would go along with the probability that it wouldn't. (See p. 32.)

5 When Michael walked along a paved road, he deliberately walked on the cracks in the pavement. As he did so, he rehearsed the belief that he didn't have to know for sure that his family was safe. This helped him to accept the probability that they were safe and that walking on the cracks had no bearing on their safety. (See p. 32.)

6 Mary was concerned about talking in small groups, but rather than remain silent she spoke up at every reasonable opportunity. In doing so, she looked at everyone while covertly rehearsing the belief that she could accept herself even if they showed disapproval. (See p. 33.)

7 Roger is concerned about travelling on the underground in case he has certain thoughts on the train. Roger still travels on the underground and makes no attempt to distract himself from these thoughts. In doing so, he rehearses the belief that he doesn't have to be in full control of his thoughts. (See p. 33.)

8 Brian refrains from overpreparing for his presentation, but instead spends an appropriate amount of time in preparing for his contribution. (See pp. 33–4.)

9 Daphne wanted to overcome her hypochondriasis. So she

rehearsed the concern-related belief that she did not have to know that she was not suffering from skin cancer. This helped her to see that not knowing did not mean that she had cancer. Behaviourally, she refrained from constantly checking for small changes in her skin and only went to her doctor if it had not improved after a week. She also stopped showing her friends her blemishes. (See pp. 34–5.)

10 Peter suffered from unhealthy jealousy and wanted to do something about it. So he practised a concern-related belief (i.e. 'I don't have to know if Stephanie finds other men attractive and if she does I can still accept myself. I don't have to be the only man in the world that Stephanie finds attractive'). Behaviourally, when Peter watched TV with Stephanie and thought that she might find a man on the screen attractive, he refrained from asking Stephanie if she found this man attractive. (See p. 35.)

11 Gerald, a lecturer, received an anonymous complaint written by one of his students and was asked by his head of department to write a reply. Rather than write the letter straight away, his concern-related belief encouraged him to give the matter a great deal of consideration and he decided to involve his union at an early stage. In doing so, he avoided making errors that he might have made if he had acted impulsively, which he may well have done if he held an anxiety-related belief about the threat. (See p. 34.)

In the previous chapter, I showed you that when you act in ways that are consistent with your anxiety, then the responses that you get from your physical and social environment often reinforce this anxiety-based behaviour and deprive you of opportunities of identifying, challenging and changing your anxiety-related beliefs. When you act in ways that are consistent with your concern-related beliefs, because this behaviour is frequently constructive, it elicits responses from your physical and social environment which reinforce this constructive behaviour.

To recap, in this chapter I discussed the nature of concern. In particular, I showed that we are largely concerned about what we perceive to be realistic threats to important aspects of our personal domain (both ego and non-ego). I then went on to consider the central role that general and specific concern-related beliefs play in concern anxiety, and in doing so I discussed the four major forms that our concern-related beliefs take (full preference beliefs, anti-awfulizing beliefs, high frustration tolerance beliefs and self-acceptance beliefs) before outlining the emotional, thinking and behavioural consequences of these beliefs.

In the next two chapters, I will show you how you can overcome ego anxiety (Chapter 3) and non-ego anxiety (Chapter 4). If you think that your anxiety problems are mainly to do with self-esteem issues, go on to Chapter 3, but if you think that your problems are mainly in the non-ego area go straight to Chapter 4 (see pp. 16–20 to help you decide where your anxiety problems mainly lie). Chapters 3 and 4 share the same structure, so you won't lose out if you only read one of the two chapters. If you think that your anxiety problems are in both areas, read both chapters and Chapter 5, where I discuss how ego anxiety and non-ego anxiety interact, sometimes in complex ways.

3

Overcoming Ego Anxiety

In this chapter, I am going to show you how to overcome ego anxiety. This is the anxiety that you feel when you face an imminent threat to your ego, or self-esteem. I am going to show you how to identify your ego general anxiety-related beliefs (ego GABs) and ego specific anxiety-related beliefs (ego SABs) and how to formulate healthy ego general concern-related alternative beliefs (ego GCBs) and healthy ego specific concern-related beliefs (ego SCBs). I will also help you to deal with any remaining reservations you may have about adopting your ego GCBs and SCBs. I will then show you how you can understand the effect of your ego general anxiety-related and ego general concern-related beliefs on your threat-related inferences that you make in specific situations. Next, I will point out how you can deal with specific episodes of anxiety with special reference to changing your ego specific anxiety-related beliefs, questioning your inferences, both those that trigger your ego specific anxiety-related beliefs and those that stem from these same beliefs. I will then go on to stress the importance of acting on your ego concern-related beliefs before concluding the chapter by urging you to refrain from using unproductive thinking strategies in dealing with your anxiety.

Dealing with ego general anxiety-related beliefs

As I discussed in Chapter 1, general anxiety-related beliefs are beliefs that you hold about certain classes of events that render you vulnerable to experiencing anxiety in specific situations. They do this by leading you to infer the existence of threat in these situations, often in the absence of objective evidence that such threat exists; and by being the breeding ground for the development of specific anxiety-related beliefs which underpin situational anxiety. In this chapter, I will deal with ego general anxiety-related beliefs (GABs), while in the following chapter I will deal with non-ego GABs.

Identify your ego general anxiety-related beliefs
The first step in dealing with your ego GABs is to identify them. So how can you tell if you have an ego GAB? There are a number of

ways to determine this. Before I review these ways, let me remind you what an ego general anxiety-related belief is. An ego GAB has two main components. First, it has a theme relevant to your attitude towards yourself that is likely to span a number of situations. Second, the nature of the belief is that it is rigid and extreme. In ego anxiety, such a belief is most frequently comprised of a demanding component and a self-depreciation component.

Identify the theme of your ego GABs

In order to identify the theme of your ego GABs, you will need to review the kinds of situations you make yourself anxious about, and I will presently list a number of questions that you need to ask yourself in each of the major areas where ego anxiety is prevalent. In listing these questions, I have paid particular emphasis on one important issue. When you have ego anxiety, you hold a self-depreciation belief. Now, it is important for you to ask yourself whether you depreciate yourself mainly because you have acted, or failed to act, in a way that you disapprove or because of how others will view you for your behaviour. In some cases, it will be clear which of these two issues is at the root of your anxiety, whereas in other cases it won't be very clear which of the two is at the root. In the latter case you will need to review recent and/or vivid anxiety-based episodes to determine whether you or other people are the evaluators whose judgement you fear. In yet other cases, it will be clear to you that you fear your own judgement and that of other people. If so, you need to determine which of these two sets of judgements poses the bigger threat.

Here are the questions that I suggest you ask yourself.

1 **Failure**
   • Do you feel anxious about failure?
   • If you do, what kinds of tasks are you anxious about failing?
   • If you fail, are you more anxious about how you think of yourself or how others will think of you? If the latter, who are these other people and what do you think they will think of you for failing?
2 **Poor performance**
   • Do you feel anxious about performing poorly?
   • If so, in which areas?
   • If you do perform poorly, are you more anxious about how you think of yourself or how others will think of you? If the

latter, who are these other people and what do you think they will think of you for performing poorly?

3 *Not being loved/liked*
- Do you feel anxious about others not loving you or not liking you?
- If so, who are these other people?
- When you are anxious, why do you think these other people will not love or like you? Here, be specific about any behaviours and/or characteristics that you think these others will focus on.

4 *Being rejected*
- Do you feel anxious about being rejected?
- If so, who by?
- When you are anxious, why do you think these other people will reject you? Be specific about any behaviours/characteristics they will reject you for.

5 *Being criticized*
- Do you feel anxious about being criticized?
- If so, who by?
- When you are anxious, what do you think these people will criticize you for? Again, be specific.

6 *Being disapproved*
- Do you feel anxious about being disapproved?
- If so, who by?
- When you are anxious, why do you think these people will disapprove of you? Be specific.

7 *Someone you value preferring another to you*
- Do you feel anxious about someone you value preferring another to you?
- Who is the person (or people) you value?
- Who do you think the other will prefer?
- How do you envisage this happening?
- Why do you think the person you value would prefer the other person to you?

8 *Not having something you value which someone else has*
- Do you feel anxious about discovering that someone has something you value that you don't have?
- What kind of things do you covet?
- Which people are you likely to feel envious of?

9 *Acting poorly in public*
- Do you feel anxious about acting poorly in public?

- If so, what are you anxious about doing?
- Who are you anxious about acting poorly in front of?
- Are you more anxious about how you think of yourself or about how others will think of you?

10 *Failing to achieve your ideal*
- Do you feel anxious if you think you are about to fail to achieve one or more of your ideals?
- If so, list these ideals?
- If you do fail to live up to your ideals, are you more anxious about how you think of yourself or about how others will think of you? If the latter, who are these other people and what do you think they will think of you for failing to live up to your ideals?

Here are some illustrative themes that people regularly discover when answering these questions.

I tend to be anxious about:

- the prospect of failing to do well at work (I am more anxious about my judgement than the judgement of other people here);
- performing poorly at work and letting other people in my team down (I am more anxious about my judgement than the judgement of other people here);
- not being liked by people I admire;
- being rejected by friends for not being intellectual enough;
- being criticized by male authority figures;
- being disapproved by my mates for not being manly;
- my girlfriend of the moment flirting with other men;
- hearing that people at work may be doing better than me;
- saying stupid things in formal gatherings;
- eating high-fat foods when I am on a low-fat diet (I am more anxious about my judgement than the judgement of other people here).

Add the anxiety-related belief components to the themes

By identifying the themes of your ego general anxiety-related beliefs, you have done most of the hard work. All you have to do now is to add two anxiety-related belief components. While ego anxiety may be underpinned by a demanding belief, an awfulizing belief, an LFT belief and a self-depreciating belief, most frequently the demanding belief and the self-depreciating belief are found in ego anxiety. By adding these two components to the illustrative themes that I have just presented, we get these individuals' ego general anxiety-related beliefs:

- I must do well at work, and if I don't, I am a failure.
- I must not perform poorly at work and let other people in my team down, and if I do, this proves that I am not good enough.
- I must be liked by people I admire, and if I'm not, I'm not likeable.
- I must not be rejected by friends for not being intellectual enough, and if I am, this proves that I am a nerd.
- I must not be criticized by male authority figures, and if I am, I'm an idiot.
- I must not be disapproved by my mates for not being manly, and if I am, I'm a wimp.
- My girlfriend of the moment must not flirt with other men, and if she does, this proves that I am unlovable.
- I must not hear that people at work are doing better than me, and if I do, I'm less worthy than them.
- I must not say stupid things in formal gatherings, and if I do, I am stupid.
- I must not eat high-fat foods when I am on a low-fat diet, and if I do, I'm a greedy pig.

There are two points that I want to make at this stage:

1 Ego general anxiety-related beliefs may be expressed in either 'I must . . .' or 'I must not . . .' form. Sometimes these two forms are interchangeable, but not always. For example, if you hold the following ego GAB: 'I must be accepted by my peers', this is not the same as holding the ego GAB 'I must not be rejected by my peers.' Imagine that your peers show neither that they accept you nor that they reject you. You will be anxious about this situation if you believe 'I must be accepted by my peers' because they haven't shown you that they accept you (i.e. this is a threat for you), but you won't be anxious about it if you believe 'I must not be rejected by my peers' because they haven't shown that they reject you (i.e. this isn't a threat for you). So give careful thought about which of these two forms best reflects each of your ego GABs.

2 Ego general anxiety-related beliefs vary with respect to how general they are. For example, let's take one of the beliefs listed

above: 'I must be liked by people whom I admire and if I'm not, I'm not likeable.' Let me now place this belief in a hierarchy which shows beliefs that are more general than it (placed above this belief) and less general than it (placed below this belief).

'I must be liked by everybody and if I'm not, I'm unlikeable'	More general
'I must be liked by everybody who is significant to me and if I'm not, I'm unlikeable'	↑
'I must be liked by people I admire and if I'm not, I'm unlikeable'	—
'I must be liked by older people I admire and if I'm not, I'm unlikeable'	
'I must be liked by older men I admire and if I'm not, I'm unlikeable'	↓ Less general

As you can see, as we go up the hierarchy the belief contains fewer restrictions. Thus, in the top belief, the person demands that everybody must like him and so if any person dislikes him he views himself as unlikeable. Contrast this with the bottom belief, where the person demands that all older men he admires must like him and if one of this more restricted group dislikes him he views himself as unlikeable. Bear this point in mind as you formulate your general anxiety-related beliefs.

Formulate your alternative ego general concern-related belief

The next step in dealing with your ego GABs is to formulate an alternative general concern-related belief for each of them. These alternative beliefs are known as ego general concern-related beliefs (or ego GCBs). If you recall from Chapter 2, the healthy alternatives to the demanding and self-depreciation components of anxiety-related beliefs are known as full preferences and self-acceptance beliefs. You will need to include both of these components when you formulate your ego GCBs. Here are the alternative general concern-related beliefs to those general anxiety-related beliefs listed above.

- I want to do well at work, but I don't have to do so. If I don't, I am not a failure; rather, I am a fallible human being who can succeed and fail.

69

- I'd much prefer it if I did not perform poorly at work and let other people in my team down, but I am not immune from doing so. If I do, this does not prove that I am not good enough. It proves that I am a fallible human being who can perform well and poorly.
- I want to be liked by people I admire, but I don't have to be. If I'm not, it doesn't prove that I am unlikeable. It proves that I am a fallible human being who can be liked by some and disliked by others, and who has likeable and dislikeable features.
- I'd rather not be rejected by friends for not being intellectual enough, but I'm not exempt from such rejection. If I am rejected, it does not prove that I am a nerd. It proves that I am a fallible human being who can be rejected and accepted by people, and who can be viewed as intellectual enough by some and not by others.
- I don't want to be criticized by male authority figures, but that doesn't mean that I must not be criticized by them. If I am, it does not mean that I am an idiot. Rather, it means that I am a fallible human being who is capable of doing things that can be praised and criticized by this group.
- I'd prefer not to be disapproved by my mates for not being manly, but there is no law of nature that states that I must not be so disapproved. If I am it does not mean that I am a wimp. It means that I am a fallible human being who can be viewed as manly and unmanly by my mates, and who can have manly and unmanly features.
- I don't want my girlfriend of the moment to flirt with other men, but that doesn't mean that she mustn't. If she does, this does not prove that I am unlovable. It proves that I am a human being whose worth isn't dependent upon how my girlfriend of the moment behaves. I am worthy because I am alive, human and fallible.
- I don't want to hear that people at work are doing better than me, but that doesn't mean that I mustn't hear this. If I do, it does not mean that I am less worthy than them. I am equal in worth to them whether they do better than me or I do better than them.
- I don't want to say stupid things in formal gatherings, but I am not exempt from doing so. If I do, I am not stupid; rather, I am a fallible human being who can say intelligent things, stupid things and neutral things in formal gatherings.
- I'd rather not eat high-fat foods when I am on a low-fat diet, but I am not immune from doing so. If I do, I am not a greedy pig;

rather I am a fallible human being who at times has difficulty sticking to a diet.

Question both sets of beliefs

The next step is for you to question both of these beliefs. While there are a number of ways in which you can do this, I suggest that you do so by considering both your ego GAB and your ego GCB at the same time and by answering three questions. Let me first list these questions and then illustrate their use.

Question 1: Which of these two beliefs is true and which is false? Give reasons for your answer.
Question 2: Which of these two beliefs is logical and which is illogical? Give reasons for your answer.
Question 3: Which of these two beliefs yields largely healthy results and which yields largely unhealthy results? Give reasons for your answer.

I have discussed why anxiety-related beliefs (in this case comprising demanding beliefs and self-depreciation beliefs) are false, illogical and largely unconstructive, in Chapter 1, and why concern-related beliefs (in this case comprising full preference beliefs and self-acceptance beliefs) are true, logical and largely constructive, in Chapter 2, and I suggest that you review this material before proceeding.

In the following example I will show you how Erica questioned her ego GAB ('I must not say stupid things in formal gatherings and if I do I am stupid') and her alternative ego GCB ('I don't want to say stupid things in formal gatherings, but I am not exempt from doing so. If I do, I am not stupid; rather I am a fallible human being who can say intelligent things, stupid things and neutral things in formal gatherings') using the above three questions.

71

Erica's ego GAB

I must not say stupid things in formal gatherings and if I do, I am stupid.

Erica's ego GCB

I don't want to say stupid things in formal gatherings, but I am not exempt from doing so. If I do, I am not stupid; rather I am a fallible human being who can say intelligent things, stupid things and neutral things in formal gatherings.

Question 1: Which of these two beliefs is true and which is false? Give reasons for your answer.

Answer 1: My ego GCB is true and my ego GAB is false. Let me first compare the demanding component of my ego GAB with the full preference component of my ego GCB. If the demanding component were true, i.e. that I must not say stupid things in formal gatherings, then there is no way that I could say stupid things in such settings because my behaviour would be governed by that law of nature. It is obvious that no such law exists because it is perfectly possible for me to say stupid things in public. I don't want to do so, that's true, but I can. And it is also true from what I have said above that I am not exempt from saying stupid things in public. So, the full preference component of my ego GCB is true.

Now let me compare the self-depreciation component of my ego GAB with the self-acceptance component of my ego GCB. 'I am stupid' doesn't mean that I have acted stupidly, it means that stupid defines my identity, that I am a stupid person for saying stupid things in formal gatherings. But if I was truly a stupid person, then I could only act stupidly, not just in formal gatherings but in all situations. Obviously that is not true. Rather, I can prove that I am a fallible human being and I can prove that I am able to say all kinds of things in formal gatherings, not just stupid things.

For all these reasons, my ego GAB is false and my ego GCB is true.

Question 2: Which of these two beliefs is logical and which is illogical? Give reasons for your answer.

Answer 2: My ego GAB is illogical and my ego GCB belief is logical. These two beliefs have two components and I will answer this question by considering these components one at a time. Let me first consider the demanding component and the full preference component. Both of these components are based on a partial preference, i.e. 'I don't want to say stupid things in formal gatherings.' This belief is flexible.

Now, my full preference belief *both* asserts what I don't want to happen (i.e. 'I don't want to say stupid things in formal gatherings . . .') *and* negates my demands ('. . . but I am not exempt from doing so'). Both of these belief elements are flexible and are therefore logically connected together. Therefore, the full preference component of my ego GCB is logical. My demand, however, asserts both what I don't want to happen (i.e. 'I don't want to say stupid things in formal gatherings . . .') and my demand ('. . . therefore I must not do so'). The first element of this demanding belief is flexible and the second is rigid. Therefore, my demanding belief is illogical because it contains an illogical non sequitur, in that you cannot logically derive something rigid from something flexible.

I recommend that you show this diagrammatically. Figure 1 shows what Erica's diagram looked like.

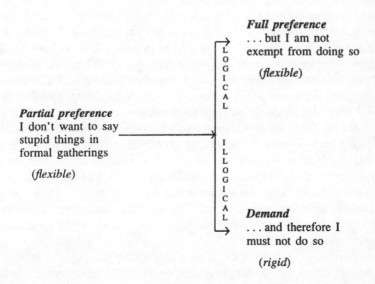

Figure 1

Second, my self-depreciation belief is illogical and my self-acceptance belief is logical. My self-depreciation belief says that if a part of me is stupid (i.e. saying stupid things at formal gatherings) then the whole of me is stupid. This is an example of an illogicality that philosophers refer to as the part–whole error. However, my self-acceptance belief avoids this error. By saying that the whole of me is fallible and made up of intelligent things, stupid things and non-stupid things, it is logical for me to say that when a part of me is stupid then this part cannot define me, but is incorporated within the wider 'whole' view of myself.

Question 3: Which of these two beliefs yields largely healthy results and which yields largely unhealthy results? Give reasons for your answer.

Answer 3: My ego GAB is largely unconstructive and will mainly give me poor results. Thus, when I have to attend formal gatherings, it will lead me to focus on the threatening aspects of the situation, e.g. that I am bound to say stupid things and that people present are bound to think negatively about me, in the absence of evidence that either of these things will happen. It will lead me to feel anxious about the prospect of attending such gatherings and it will influence for the worse my behaviour in these situations, e.g. it may lead me to avoid attending these gatherings at the last minute, to withdraw from them before I act stupidly or to try to be invisible if I stay by staying silent or by agreeing with everyone. Finally, it will lead me to think of the dire consequences of acting stupidly. Thus, I will think that everyone will remember my behaviour for a long time and discuss me behind my back or that I will be shunned in future.

My ego GCB is, however, largely constructive and will mainly give me good results. Thus, when I have to attend formal gatherings, it will lead me to focus on the objective aspects of the situation and will only lead me to think that I am facing threat if objectively I am, e.g. if I know little about a subject and am expected to speak authoritatively on it. It will lead me to feel concerned about the prospect of attending such gatherings when I am facing a realistic threat and it will influence for the better my behaviour in these situations, e.g. it will lead me to go to such gatherings, to stay in them even if the going gets tough, to speak up if I have something to say and to disagree with people. Finally, it will lead me to think realistically of the consequences of acting stupidly. Thus, I will think some may remember my behaviour for a long time, but that most will soon forget it, that some may talk about me behind my back, but that most won't, and that it is highly unlikely that I will be shunned in future for acting stupidly.

Decide which set of beliefs you want to live by

Having questioned both your ego GAB and your ego GCB, the next stage is for you to decide which of these beliefs you wish to live by. If you have questioned your beliefs comprehensively, it should be clear to you that your life will be enriched by your ego GCB and hampered by your ego GAB and that your decision is clear cut.

However, it may be that you are reluctant to commit yourself fully to your ego GCB because you have some objections to it or some reservations/doubts about living your life according to it. You may also consider that your ego GAB has some advantages that you may lose if you commit yourself to your ego GCB or that there are negative consequences to adopting the ego GCB. If any of these are the case, then it is important for you to be clear with yourself about what these objections, reservations, doubts, losses and negative consequences are so that you can determine whether they are realistic or distorted.

Here is a list of Erica's objections, etc., and how she responded to them.

1 *If I commit myself to my ego GCB then I will increase the chances that I will say stupid things in public*
   Response: Actually, the opposite is probably true. Since my ego GAB leads to anxiety it increases the chances of me saying stupid things in public because I won't think very clearly about what I am saying. My ego GCB helps me to focus on what I say rather than how I am coming across to people and thus decreases the chances that I will say stupid things.
2 *If I give up my ego GAB then I will become complacent and not care what I say in formal gatherings*
   Response: If I give up my ego GAB and replace it with an attitude of indifference then I may not care what I say in formal gatherings. However, if I replace it with my ego GCB then I will still care about what I say without being anxiously preoccupied about it.
3 *The idea of telling myself that I am fallible is an excuse for me acting stupidly*
   Response: No, it's not. It's a reason. I can accept myself as

fallible and still take responsibility for what I say in formal gatherings.

In this way, Erica dealt with all her obstacles, etc., about committing herself to her ego GCB, which she duly did. In the same way, after you have questioned both your ego GAB and ego GCB, identify and deal with the perceived obstacles, doubts, reservations, losses and costs that you associate with giving up the former and committing yourself to the latter. When you have done so, you are ready for the next step in your overcoming anxiety programme.

Before I go on to describe this step, I want to emphasize one important point. In order to change your ego GABs to ego GCBs you need to question both sets of beliefs repeatedly. I suggest that you do so 20 minutes a day using the three questions listed above. Then spend some time responding to any doubts, reservations, etc., that you have about committing yourself to holding your ego GCBs. This repeated practice is a vital part of acquiring a concern-based philosophy and becoming more realistic in inferring the actual existence of threat.

Understand the relationship between threat and your general ego beliefs

In Chapters 1 and 2, I discussed the impact of holding general anxiety-related beliefs and concern-related beliefs on inferences of threat. Basically, I showed that when you bring your general anxiety-related beliefs to relevant situations, you tend to focus on the threatening aspects of the situation that are consistent with the content of the GABs, whereas when you bring your general concern-related beliefs to the same relevant situations, you are much more realistic in the inferences that you make about these situations and only consider that threat is imminent when it is objectively clear that it is.

Thus, after you have questioned your ego GAB and your ego GCB and have committed yourself to the latter, it is useful to be aware of the kinds of inferences that you are likely to make when holding each belief. Why? Because this will help you to view situations that you have previously seen as full of threat more realistically.

This is what happened when Erica did this:

Erica's ego GAB
I must not say stupid things in formal gatherings and if I do, I am stupid.

Erica's ego GCB
I don't want to say stupid things in formal gatherings, but I am not exempt from doing so. If I do, I am not stupid; rather I am a fallible human being who can say intelligent things, stupid things and neutral things in formal gatherings.

This belief leads me to infer

This belief leads me to infer

1 There is a very good chance that I will say stupid things in formal gatherings.

1 I may say stupid things in formal gatherings if I have to speak about something I don't know about. Otherwise, I will talk intelligently.

2 Everyone will notice because I will say very stupid things.

2 If I say stupid things, it is likely that they will only be a little bit stupid rather than very stupid and thus not everyone will notice.

3 People will think that I am stupid for saying stupid things.

3 If I do say stupid things, some people may think that I am stupid for saying them, but most won't label me in this way.

4 People will stop inviting me to social gatherings for saying stupid things.

4 Some people may stop inviting me to social gatherings for saying stupid things, but most will continue to issue such invitations.

Having become aware of the effect of your ego GAB and your ego GCB on your inferences, it is important to apply this knowledge. Let me put this step into the overall context of dealing with one of your ego GABs.

Step 1 Identify your ego GAB and its healthy alternative (ego GCB).

Step 2 Question both beliefs.

Step 3 Commit yourself to your ego GCB, having dealt with any objections, reservations, etc., to so doing.

Step 4 Become aware of the impact of both of these beliefs on the inferences that you are likely to make about relevant situations.

Step 5 Once you have become aware of anxiety-based inferences, label them as such and challenge the ego GAB that underpins them.

(Every time Erica thought about going to a formal gathering and began to focus on her anxiety-based inferences – listed on the left-hand side of the above diagram – she challenged her ego GAB.)

Step 6 Actively hold your ego GCB beliefs and focus on the inferences that stem from them.

(Erica then actively rehearsed her ego GCB and focused on the concern-based inferences – listed on the right-hand side of the above diagram.)

Step 7 If you need to challenge your anxiety-based inferences by asking and answering questions designed to assess how realistic the inferences are, here are some suggestions:

- How likely is it that . . . ?
- Would an objective jury agree that . . . ? If not, how would they view it?
- Am I viewing the situation realistically? If not, how can I view it more realistically?

It is important that you practise these steps regularly if you are to develop your ego GCBs and the realistic thinking about situations you have previously viewed as full of threat.

The major goal of the interventions that I have focused on in this section is to help you to develop healthy ego GCBs so that you can view relevant situations more realistically and are less likely to see threat where none objectively exists. In the next section, I will show you how you can overcome your anxiety in specific situations if you think (realistically or not) that threat is imminent.

Dealing with specific episodes of ego anxiety by changing your specific ego anxiety-related beliefs

If you develop general concern-based beliefs in relation to yourself (i.e. ego GCBs), you will generally be more realistic in inferring the presence of imminent threat to your self-esteem. However, even if you do this, at times you will still be anxious about specific threats either because your inference about facing threat is accurate or because you may still occasionally think you are facing threat when you are not. As I explained in Chapter 1, when you experience anxiety in specific situations this is because you hold a specific anxiety-related belief in that situation. In this section, then, I will show how you can overcome specific episodes of ego anxiety largely by changing your specific ego anxiety-related beliefs (ego SABs) to specific ego concern-related beliefs (ego SCBs). The first step in this process is to discover why you are feeling anxiety in the specific situation under consideration. You can do this by using REBT's famous ABC framework.

Using the ABC framework

When dealing with ego anxiety in specific situations, the best way to use the ABC framework is as follows:

Situation = A description of the situation in which you are anxious
A = Threat (what you find most threatening in the situation)
B = Specific unhealthy beliefs about A (in ego anxiety these are most likely to be a specific demanding belief and a specific self-depreciation belief)
C (Emotional consequence of A×B) = Anxiety

Let me use Brian's example that I first discussed in Chapter 1:

Situation: Being told that I will have to make a presentation in front of my peers and my boss in a week's time
A (Threat): There is a good chance that I will not come across well to my peers and to my boss in this presentation
B (Specific unhealthy belief): I must come across well to my peers and to my boss in this presentation and I am an inadequate person if I don't.
C (Emotional consequence of **A×B**): Anxiety

The most difficult part of understanding your specific ego anxiety is pinpointing the aspect of the situation that you find most threatening. If this is the case, you might find it helpful to ask yourself the following question:

'In this situation, what one thing would take my anxiety away?'

The opposite of this answer is what you are most anxious about in the specific situation under consideration. You regard this event as something that will definitely or probably occur.

Thus, let's suppose that Brian knew he was anxious when he was informed that he had to make a presentation in front of his peers and his boss in a week's time, but he didn't know why. So he asked himself the question: 'In this situation, what one thing would take my anxiety away?' His answer was: 'Coming across well to my peers and to my boss in this presentation'. Thus, Brian was most anxious about not coming across well to his peers and to his boss in this presentation, a threat which he considered to be probable in its occurrence.

Once you have assessed the ABCs of your specific anxiety, you may be tempted to question A. However, at this stage, it is important that you assume temporarily that A is true. This enables you to challenge and change the ego SAB which underpins your ego anxiety in the specific situation in question. Thus, Brian assumed temporarily that there was a good chance that he would not come across well to his peers and to his boss in his forthcoming presentation. This enabled him to move on to the next step, which was to question his ego SAB and alternative ego SCB.

Question both sets of specific beliefs

After you have identified your ego SAB, it is important to formulate the specific ego concern-related alternative to this belief. This is known as your ego SCB. Then you can question these two beliefs in the same way as you questioned your ego GAB and ego GCB, i.e. at the same time, by answering the following three questions:

Question 1: Which of these two beliefs is true and which is false? Give reasons for your answer.
Question 2: Which of these two beliefs is logical and which is illogical? Give reasons for your answer.

Question 3: Which of these two beliefs yields largely healthy results and which yields largely unhealthy results? Give reasons for your answer.

Your answers should be similar to those that you gave when you questioned your general ego anxiety-related beliefs and your general ego concern-related beliefs, with one important exception. Your answers should be specific, since you are questioning specific healthy and unhealthy ego beliefs.

At the end of this questioning procedure it should be clear to you that your ego SAB is false, illogical and unhealthy while your ego SCB is true, logical and healthy, and that if you want to overcome your ego anxiety in the situation in question and to feel healthily concerned instead, then you need to adopt your ego SCB and relinquish your ego SAB. Once again, if you have any doubts or reservations about this, deal with them in the same way as you dealt with your doubts and reservations about relinquishing your general ego anxiety-related belief and adopting your general ego concern-related belief (see pp. 75–6).

Brian took his ego SAB ('I must come across well to my peers and to my boss in this presentation and I am an inadequate person if I don't') and formulated the alternative ego SCB ('I want to come across well to my peers and to my boss, but I don't have to do so. If I don't this does not prove that I am an inadequate person. Rather, I am a fallible human being who didn't do as well as I wanted on this occasion'). He then questioned these beliefs and clearly saw that his ego SCB was true, logical and helpful to him while his ego SAB was false, illogical and unhelpful. His one reservation about committing himself to his ego SCB was that it might lead to him becoming complacent in his preparation for the presentation. However, he realized on reflection that this was unlikely because this belief stressed his strong desire to do well in his presentation, which meant that it was very unlikely that he would be complacent in his preparation.

In order to change your ego SABs to ego SCBs you need to question both sets of beliefs repeatedly. I suggest that you do so 20 minutes a day. First, imagine that you are about to face the specific threat at A, and once you have done this keep it clearly in mind as you question these specific beliefs using the three questions listed above. Then spend some time responding to any doubts, reservations, etc., that you have about committing yourself to holding your ego SCBs. This repeated practice is a vital part of overcoming your specific ego anxiety.

Question threat at A

Once you have challenged your ego SAB and have increased your conviction in your ego SCB, it is important that you go back and consider how realistic your threat-related inference is at A. You can do this by asking the same questions that I listed on p. 78. Here they are again:

- How likely is it that . . . ?
- Would an objective jury agree that . . . ? If not, how would they view it?
- Am I viewing the situation realistically? If not, how can I view it more realistically?

Brian asked himself these questions after questioning his specific beliefs while holding his ego SCB. He took his threat at A (i.e. 'There is a good chance that I will not come across well to my peers and to my boss in this presentation'), questioned it and realized two things: that he was overestimating the probability that he wouldn't do well in the presentation, and that he was underestimating his ability to prepare well and speak well on the day. These realizations helped Brian to reinterpret his inference at A, thus: 'Although I may not come across well to my peers and to my boss in my upcoming presentation, this is very unlikely if I prepare well for it.' Brian really saw that holding an ego GCB and an ego SCB lead to accurate inferences about threat, while holding an ego GAB and an ego SAB lead to overestimation of threat. It is very important that you learn this same lesson, and the best way of doing so is to first challenge your own ego GAB and ego SAB, replace them with an alternative ego GCB and an alternative ego SCB, and question your inference at A while holding this ego SCB.

Deal with thinking consequences of ego SABs

Questioning inferences while holding an ego SCB rather than an ego SAB is also particularly important when dealing with the thinking consequences of ego SABs. Indeed, it is more important to do this when questioning these thinking consequences than it is when questioning inferences at A, for inferences at A are perhaps more determined by ego GABs than by ego SABs, while thinking consequences of ego SABs, as the term makes clear, are largely determined by those SABs.

In Chapter 1, I showed that when you hold a specific anxiety-related belief about a specific threat then this belief will not only affect your emotions and behaviour, it will also influence the way you subsequently think about the situation you are facing in ways which increase the threat content. When you do not understand this you tend to see these new increased threats as real and then bring your anxiety-related beliefs to these new As, with the result that your anxiety level is increased. This explains why people can 'work themselves into' an intense state of anxiety and panic (see pp. 26–7 for a full example of this process in Brian's case.) When this process occurs in ego anxiety, the thinking consequences of your ego SABs (which are the new increased threats) are likely to reflect the following:

1 even more negative behaviour on your part;
2 increased levels of social disapproval;
3 even more negative practical consequences in line with 1 and 2.

Thus, once Brian's ego SAB about specific threat (i.e. what he saw as the probability of not coming across well to his peers and to his boss in the specific presentation) was activated, then he began to think in ways that elaborated the threat in his mind. Thus, he began to think that:

1 'I will give one of the worst presentations ever given at these events
2 'Everyone will laugh at me'
3 'My boss will give me a very bad report at my next appraisal'

There are four ways of dealing with these thinking consequences of ego SABs.

1 Label them as thinking consequences of an ego SAB and then challenge and change this belief. Then you can go back and evaluate how realistic these thoughts are (if you need to) using the questions that I listed on p. 82.
2 Recognize that they are a sign that your anxiety is beginning to get out of control and that you need to use the ABC framework to gain control and understand what you were anxious about in the

first place. In particular, you might find it helpful to ask yourself the following question: 'In this situation, what one thing would take my anxiety away?' As I showed you earlier, the opposite of this answer is what you are most anxious about in the specific situation under consideration. This definite or probably occurring event constitutes the A in the ABC framework, anxiety constitutes the C, and this is all you need to identify your ego SAB which you then go on to question in the normal way.

3 Take one of these thinking consequences, treat it as an A and do another ABC assessment on it. Then identify and question your ego SAB before assessing how realistic the A is (as before).

4 Treat them as inferences (without necessarily challenging the underlying ego SAB) and ask yourself questions such as those that appear on p. 82.

Use imagery to change your ego SABs

So far I have suggested largely verbal means of questioning your ego SABs and ego SCBs with the purpose of changing the former to the latter. You can gain practice at changing your ego SABs by using your imagery modality. This technique is called rational-emotive imagery (REI) and I will now give you a set of instructions of how to use it and illustrate its use with reference to Brian's case. REI is best used to overcome specific episodes of anxiety and you need to have assessed such episodes using the ABC framework. You also should have had some experience in questioning your ego SABs and ego SCBs and have committed yourself to the latter.

Step 1 Vividly imagine the specific threat about which you are anxious.

(Brian imagined giving his presentation and not coming across well to his peers and to his boss.)

Step 2 Briefly (for about 30 seconds) allow yourself to feel anxious and rehearse your ego SAB while imagining the threat.

(Brian rehearsed his ego SAB – 'I must come across well to my peers and to my boss in this presentation and I am an inadequate person if I don't' – and allowed himself to feel anxious for 30 seconds.)

Step 3 Change your ego SAB to your ego SCB while all the time vividly imagining the threat, and allow yourself to feel concerned but not anxious about it.

(Brian changed his ego SAB to his ego SCB – 'I want to come across well to my peers and to my boss, but I don't have to do so. If I don't then I am not inadequate, but a fallible human being with strengths and weaknesses who is not coming across well on this occasion' – while vividly imagining himself not coming across well to them during the presentation. He felt concerned as a result.)

Step 4 Stay with the feeling of concern and the associated ego SCB while continuing to imagine the threat for ten minutes. Actively rehearse this belief if you find yourself getting anxious again.
(Brian did this.)

Step 5 Repeat Steps 1–4 formally three times a day for about 15 minutes on each occasion and at other times when you begin to think about the threat and begin to get anxious about it. When this happens, use your feelings of anxiety as a cue to practise REI.
(Brian also did this.)

You may be wondering why I suggest that you briefly allow yourself to feel anxious while practising REI. Surely, I hear you thinking, you don't need to practise feeling anxious about the specific threat under consideration. You know that you are good at doing that! This is, of course, true. But I suggest building this brief period of feeling anxious into the technique because it reflects reality. It is unrealistic to expect that you will not from now on become anxious about the specific threat in question. Quite the opposite. But I want you to see that you can use your anxiety as a signal or cue to rehearse your ego SCB and that by doing this you can make yourself concerned about the threat rather than anxious about it.

Use coping imagery

The purpose of REI is to give you practice in your mind's eye of rehearsing your ego SCBs in the face of threats, so that you can be healthily concerned about these threats happening rather than anxious about their occurrence. It is also important that you practise rehearsing, again in your mind's eye, facing more favourable outcomes. There are two situations that I suggest you rehearse.

First, you can imagine the threat occurring and see yourself dealing productively with it in some way. Here, for example, Brian might see himself not coming across well to his peers and to his boss but then might rehearse seeing himself saying something like: 'I'm getting a bit bogged down. Can someone help me out a bit?', which was in fact what Brian chose as a constructive response in his coping imagery scenario. It is important that you choose what would be a constructive response for you (from a long- as well as a short-term perspective) rather than accept what someone else views as constructive behaviour. This form of coping imagery is best practised after you have gained from using REI on dealing with the same threat. REI helps you respond constructively to the specific threat from an emotional standpoint, while this form of coping imagery helps you to respond constructively to the threat from a behavioural perspective.

The second form of coping imagery involves you imagining doing well in the same situation, with one major difference: the situation is non-threatening. Thus, when Brian used what might be called 'success imagery', he imagined himself preparing adequately for his presentation and saw himself coming across well to his peers and to his boss. Success imagery should be practised *after* REI but should be given equal time. This is important because it aids you in developing your conviction in your general concern-related belief. Why? Because seeing yourself having success experiences re-inforces the idea that threat is not inevitable in the situation under consideration (and related situations) unless there is clear evidence that such threat exists.

Act on your ego concern-related beliefs

So far, I have shown you how to change your general and specific ego anxiety-related beliefs using your ability to think and to image. These are important steps and not to be downplayed. However, if you do not act in ways that are consistent with your general and specific ego concern-related beliefs and inconsistent with your general and specific ego anxiety-related beliefs you will not develop the former and change the latter, and thus you will neither overcome your specific anxiety problem nor become less vulnerable to ego anxiety. So action is central to overcoming anxiety, action that does not reinforce anxiety-related beliefs, but that does reinforce concern-related beliefs.

Refrain from acting on your anxiety-related action tendencies and act on your concern-related tendencies instead

In Chapter 1, I discussed various behaviours that stem from anxiety-related beliefs. These behaviours have two major components: action tendencies which, as the term makes clear, involve experiencing an urge or a tendency to act in certain ways, and overt behaviours, where you actually act on these urges or tendencies.

As I stressed earlier in this chapter, when you experience ego anxiety it is important to view this as a signal to do something about it. In fact, when you feel ego anxiety you have a choice: you can decide either to act on your action tendencies (which I shall list presently) or to challenge the ego anxiety-related beliefs which underpin your ego anxiety. Of course, I recommend that you do the latter rather than the former, even though it is much easier to do the former than the latter, and the former gets rid of feelings of ego anxiety more quickly than the latter. However, I hope you have grasped by now that getting rid of your ego anxiety feelings in the short term is not the same as overcoming your ego anxiety in the longer term. Indeed, if you act on the following anxiety-based action tendencies in the short term, you make it harder to overcome your ego anxiety in the longer term because you strengthen rather than challenge your specific and general ego anxiety-related beliefs. What do you need to do instead? After you have challenged your anxiety-related beliefs and committed yourself to the alternative concern-related beliefs, you need to translate your concern-based action tendencies into actual behaviour. In particular:

1 Refrain from avoiding situations that you find threatening. Instead, get into the mind-set of your ego SCB and confront the situation

If you do this, two things will happen:

- if the threat materializes you will gain the experience of thinking rationally about it (i.e. viewing it from the perspective of your ego SCB) and of acting constructively as a result;
- if the threat doesn't materialize you will still have gained the experience of thinking rationally in case it occurred, and you will have realized that your inference of threat was unrealistic.

You do need to be sensible in confronting threat. Confronting too much threat too soon may not be good for you because you may not be able to use your developing self-help skills in such 'overwhelming' situations. On the other hand, going too slowly in confronting threat may reinforce your unhealthy and unrealistic view that you are fragile and need protection from a harsh world. For these reasons I normally suggest that when you confront threat, you do so according to a principle I have called 'challenging, but not overwhelming'.

This involves you developing a hierarchy of situations that you find threatening, from the smallest threat at the bottom to the biggest at the top. You then confront the threat that you find a challenge, but not one that you would find 'overwhelming' at that time, nor one that you would not find a challenge to face. If you apply this principle and practise your ego SCBs as you do so, you will find that you make reasonably quick progress up your hierarchy of threatening situations. There are exceptions to this 'challenging, but not overwhelming', as in the treatment of phobias and post-traumatic stress disorder, but these fall outside the scope of this book. If you have a phobia or think you may be suffering from PTSD, in the first instance see your doctor who will, if necessary, make a specialist referral.

2 Don't withdraw from threat. Stay in the situation and think rationally and act constructively

If you withdraw from a situation because you think that a threat is imminent, you may again obtain temporary relief from your anxiety, but you will not overcome your anxiety in the longer term. This is true for two reasons. First, when you withdraw you are reinforcing your ego SAB. Let's suppose that Brian was sitting in the room where he had to give his presentation and just before he was called upon to speak he thought that he would not give a good talk, which he demanded must not happen and would prove him to be inadequate if it did. If he left the room at this point, saying, for example, that he was unwell, he would be acting according to his SAB, which would thus be reinforced. Second, he would not test his inference that he would give a poor presentation.

Instead of withdrawing from a situation because you think that a threat is imminent, it is important that you remain in the situation and practise thinking rationally about the occurrence of the threat. Thus, instead of withdrawing when he suddenly thought that he might not give a good presentation, it would be important for Brian to remain in the situation and rehearse his ego SCB (i.e. that it would be desirable for him to give a good presentation, but that he doesn't have to and if he doesn't then this does not prove that he is inadequate; rather it proves that he is a complex, fallible human being with strengths and weaknesses who didn't do well on this occasion). Staying in the situation would serve to reinforce Brian's ego SCB and enable him to test his inference that he would give a poor presentation, and if he did it would help him to act constructively in the situation, e.g. by acknowledging that he was stuck and asking for help.

3 Relinquish your safety-seeking behaviours and focus your attention on the part of the situation where you anticipate threat

In Chapter 1, I discussed the concept of safety-seeking behaviours and how these help you deal with your anxiety in the short term but do not help you to overcome your anxiety in the longer term. In ego anxiety, the purpose of safety-seeking behaviours is, as the term implies, to help keep you safe from threat while remaining in the situation: safe from the threat of being aware that you are acting in ways for which you would depreciate yourself or from the threat of being viewed negatively or treated negatively by others, either of which would lead you again to depreciate yourself.

Perhaps the most common form of safety-seeking behaviour in ego anxiety is avoidance in situ. Here, you focus your attention away from where you think the threat is. In Brian's case, this would involve not looking at his audience while giving his presentation for fear of seeing them looking at him with disapproval. Indeed, 'not looking' where you think the threat might be is a very common form of avoidance in situ. Brian may get through the presentation by employing this safety-seeking behaviour, but by using it he reinforces his ego SAB (it is as if Brian is saying here: 'Since I would be inadequate if I saw that I was not coming across well to my peers and to my boss, it is best if I don't look at them'). Also, by using this safety-seeking behaviour, Brian deprives himself of the opportunity of seeing how realistic his inference (that he is not coming across well) is. In these two ways, Brian unwittingly perpetuates his ego anxiety problem and deprives himself of the opportunity of working to overcome it.

What should Brian do instead? He should hold his ego SCB and look at his audience to see whether or not he is coming across well. If he does this from the perspective of his ego SCB, then he will appraise the situation realistically and only see threat when it exists. If he looks from the perspective of his ego SAB, then he may well see threat when none objectively exists.

In general, it is important to avoid using safety-seeking behaviours and instead to focus your attention on the situation where you think that threat may be present. As you do this, make sure that you do so from the perspective of your ego SCB so that you get practice at thinking rationally about the possible existence of the threat and at viewing the part of the situation where the threat may exist realistically.

4 Stop seeking reassurance. Instead, start living with uncertainty, challenge your anxiety-related beliefs and be realistic in your inferences

When you are anxious about performing poorly or not being approved of – two common ego anxieties – you may ask others for reassurance that you have not performed poorly in the first place, or are approved of in the second. If you receive such reassurance, you feel better for a while (because the threat has been removed, albeit temporarily), but do not get over your ego anxiety because you still hold a general and specific anxiety-related belief about performing poorly or not being approved of. These beliefs will then lead you to infer that you are doing poorly or are not being approved of when these are not the case and then, because you are anxious, you seek reassurance and the entire reassurance cycle is repeated.

What should you do instead of seeking reassurance? As in other cases, I recommend that you put up with the uncertainty of not knowing for sure how you are doing or how you are viewed by others, and challenge your ego GABs and ego SABs about the possibility of performing poorly and of not being approved. Your ego GCBs and ego SCBs will then help you to be realistic in your inferences about your performance and how others view you.

5 Don't overcompensate in your behaviour, but do take sensible action

The purpose of compensatory behaviour in dealing with anxiety is to bring about the very opposite of what you fear. As I discussed in Chapter 1, if Brian were to engage in compensatory behaviour to deal with his anxiety about not coming across well to his peers and to his boss, he would overprepare his performance so that there was no chance of him doing other than brilliantly. He would try and ensure that it was the best presentation that those present had ever seen. This is the very opposite of what he fears may happen. The trouble with compensatory behaviour is that you spend all your time acting in a way to ensure that what you fear (i.e. the threat) will not happen, so that you do not spend any time identifying, challenging and changing the anxiety-related belief about the threat that underpins your anxiety.

Instead of overcompensating for your ego anxiety, challenge your ego anxiety-related beliefs, commit yourself to holding ego concern-related beliefs and take sensible action, which in Brian's case would be to prepare well for his presentation, but not to overprepare for it in order to give the best presentation his peers and boss have ever seen.

6 Stop acting impulsively to neutralize the threat and give yourself time to think in a reflective, considered manner

When you hold anxiety-related beliefs and you think that a threat to your personal domain is imminent, then you may well act very quickly to get rid of the threat. Such impulsive behaviour is likely to make matters worse because it is based on an absence of considered, reflective thinking. Such thinking allows you to consider the options that are available to you, to think of the pros and cons of each course of action and to choose the best course available to you. However, in order for you to do this, you have to view the situation from the perspective of your ego concern-related beliefs.

As you have probably gathered, I recommend the combined use of ego concern-related thinking and concern-based action as a powerful way of overcoming impulsive action. Some people say that they don't have the time to question their beliefs in the heat of the moment. This is a valid point. Consequently, I suggest that you write down your ego concern-related beliefs on 3×5 cards (one to a card) and rehearse them frequently even if you are not facing threat. In particular, consult these cue cards when you think threat is imminent. Brian's cue card read: 'I don't have to impress my peers and boss. I can accept myself if I don't.' Cue cards are frequently shortened versions of fully expressed ego concern-related beliefs, but reflect the full meaning of the longer version.

Deal with your unproductive thinking strategies

The final issue that I wish to consider in this chapter concerns the importance of refraining from using unproductive thinking strategies in dealing with your anxiety. In Chapter 1, I showed you that in order to stop yourself from becoming anxious when you suspect that a threat is on the horizon or to get rid of your anxious feelings once you have begun to experience them, you may use one or more of a number of unproductive thinking strategies, such as distraction, reassurance thinking, compensatory thinking and defensive thinking (see Chapter 1 for a full discussion of these unproductive strategies).

Instead of distracting yourself from the threat to your self-esteem, reassuring yourself that such a threat does not exist, thinking how great you are (compensatory thinking) or defending yourself from the threat, it is important that you:

1 assume temporarily that the threat to your self-esteem does exist;
2 acknowledge that you feel ego anxiety about this threat and use this as a cue to Step 3;
3 identify, challenge and change the ego SAB and replace it with your alternative ego SCB;
4 take appropriate action to strengthen your ego SCB as outlined in the previous section;
5 use problem-solving thinking in preparing to deal constructively with the threat (see Chapter 2, pp. 57–8 for a discussion of problem-solving in dealing with threat);
6 put into practice your chosen strategy for dealing constructively with the threat.

In order to take these steps you have to first:

1 Become aware of your individual unproductive thinking strategies. Use the four general headings – distraction, reassurance thinking, compensatory thinking and defensive thinking – as a guide here.
2 Acknowledge that these strategies are unproductive, see clearly why this is so and resolve to give them up.
3 Realize that giving up these strategies involves you experiencing more ego anxiety in the short term, but that this is necessary if you are to overcome your ego anxiety in the longer term. This is so because you are facing up to the threat rather than avoiding thinking about it or neutralizing it. Remember the point that an avoided or neutralized threat is an undealt-with threat.

In the next chapter, I will use the structure of this chapter to discuss how you can overcome non-ego anxiety.

4

Overcoming Non-ego Anxiety

In this chapter, I am going to show you how to overcome non-ego anxiety. This is the anxiety that you feel when you face an imminent threat to things that are important to you that do not involve your ego, or self-esteem. I am going to show you how to identify your non-ego general anxiety-related beliefs (non-ego GABs) and how to formulate healthy non-ego general concern-related alternative beliefs (non-ego GCBs). I will also help you to deal with any remaining reservations you may have about adopting your non-ego GCBs. I will then show you how you can understand the effect of your non-ego GABs and non-ego GCBs on the threat-related inferences that you make in specific situations. Next, I will point out how you can deal with specific episodes of non-ego anxiety with special reference to changing your non-ego specific anxiety-related beliefs (non-ego SABs), questioning your inferences, both those that trigger your non-ego SABs and those that stem from these same beliefs. I will then go on to stress the importance of acting on your non-ego concern-related beliefs before concluding the chapter by urging you to refrain from using unproductive thinking strategies in dealing with your non-ego anxiety.

Dealing with non-ego general anxiety-related beliefs

As I discussed in Chapter 1, general anxiety-related beliefs are beliefs that you hold about certain classes of events that render you vulnerable to experiencing anxiety in specific situations. They do this by leading you to infer the existence of threat in these situations, often in the absence of objective evidence that such threat exists, and by being the breeding ground for the development of specific anxiety-related beliefs which underpin situational anxiety. In this chapter, I will deal with non-ego general anxiety-related beliefs (non-ego GABs). In the previous chapter, I dealt with ego GABs.

Identify your non-ego general anxiety-related beliefs

The first step in dealing with your non-ego GABs is to identify them. So, how can you tell if you have a non-ego GAB? There are a number of ways to determine this. Before I review these ways, let me remind you what a non-ego general anxiety-related belief is. A non-ego GAB has two main components. It has a theme, relevant to things important to you that do not relate to your ego or self-esteem, that is likely to span a number of situations. Second, the nature of the belief is that it is rigid and extreme. In non-ego anxiety, such a belief most frequently comprises a demanding component and either an awfulizing component (where you focus more on the 'horrors' of the world: '*It* would be awful if . . .') or a low frustration tolerance (LFT) component (where you focus more on internal 'horrors': '*I* would not be able to bear it if . . .').

Identify the theme of your non-ego GABs

In order to identify the theme of your non-ego GABs, you will need to review the kinds of situations you make yourself anxious about. In Chapter 1, I listed the main non-ego themes in anxiety. Here, I will list those non-ego themes that are commonly found in non-ego anxiety along with some questions for you to answer.

1 *Frustration*
   • Do you feel anxious about being frustrated?
   • If you do, which situations are you anxious about being frustrated in?
2 *Discomfort*
   • Do you feel anxious about experiencing discomfort?
   • If so, which situations are you anxious about experiencing discomfort in?
   • What type (or types) of discomfort are you particularly anxious about experiencing?
3 *Emotional pain*
   • Do you feel anxious about feeling certain emotions?
   • If you do, which emotion or emotions do you feel particularly anxious about experiencing?
   • In which situations do you routinely experience these feared emotions?
4 *Non-ego loss*
   • Do you feel anxious about losing what is important to you?
   • If so, what or who are you anxious about losing and under which circumstances?
5 *Unfairness/injustice to self or others*
   • Do you feel anxious about encountering unfairness or injustice to yourself or to others?

- If so, what kinds of unfairness/injustice are you anxious about encountering?

6 *Loss of control*
- Do you feel anxious about losing control?
- If so, in which ways and in which situations are you scared about losing control?

7 *Uncertainty*
- Do you feel anxious when you experience uncertainty?
- Which situations in which you are uncertain are you particularly anxious about?

8 *Health/illness*
- Do you feel anxious about your health or about becoming ill?
- If so, which illnesses are you particularly scared of?
- Under which circumstances are you anxious about your health or about becoming ill?

9 *Loss of security*
- Are you anxious about losing your sense of security?
- If so, what kind of security are you anxious about losing and under which circumstances?

10 *Conflict*
- Are you anxious about conflict?
- If so, what kind of conflict are you anxious about and under which circumstances?

Here are some illustrative themes that people regularly discover when answering these questions.

I tend to be anxious about:

- being late for appointments;
- being uncomfortable when talking to people;
- being anxious in enclosed spaces;
- losing valuable possessions;
- the prospect of being treated unfairly at work;
- not being in control of my thoughts;
- not knowing whether or not my loved ones are safe;
- the possibility of getting cancer;
- my parents not being around to look after me;
- family members arguing.

Add the anxiety-related belief components to the themes

By identifying the themes of your non-ego general anxiety-related beliefs, you have done most of the hard work. All you have to do now is to add two non-ego anxiety-related belief components. Non-ego anxiety is underpinned by a demanding belief, an awfulizing belief and an LFT belief, but – by definition – not by a self-depreciating belief. Non-ego anxiety may be underpinned by a depreciation belief about others or about life conditions, but I will not deal with this issue here. When the emphasis is on external horror, then the two belief components are likely to be a demanding belief and an awfulizing belief (although an LFT belief may be found instead of an awfulizing belief), whereas when the emphasis is on internal horror and your perceived inability to bear something, then the two belief components are likely to be a demanding belief and an LFT belief (although an awfulizing belief may be found instead of an LFT belief). By adding the relevant two components to the illustrative themes that I have just presented, we get these individuals' non-ego general anxiety-related beliefs:

- I must not be late for appointments and it would be terrible if I were.
- I must not be uncomfortable when talking to people and it would be unbearable if I were.
- I must not become anxious when I am in enclosed spaces and it would be intolerable if I were.
- I must not lose any of my valuable possessions and it would be horrible if I were to.
- I must not be treated unfairly at work and it would be awful if I were to be.
- I must not lose control of my thoughts and I wouldn't be able to bear losing such control.
- I must know that my loved ones are safe and I wouldn't be able to stand not knowing.
- There must not be any possibility that I might get cancer and if there were a chance that I might get it I couldn't bear it.
- My parents must be around to look after me and it would be the end of the world if they weren't.
- Family members must not argue and I wouldn't be able to bear it if they did.

There are two points that I want to make at this stage:

1 Non-ego general anxiety-related beliefs may be expressed in either 'I must . . .' or 'I must not . . .' form. Sometimes these two

forms are interchangeable, but not always. For example, if you hold the following non-ego GAB, 'I must be treated fairly at work', this is not the same as holding the non-ego GAB, 'I must not be treated unfairly at work.' Imagine that you are treated neither fairly or unfairly at work. You will be anxious about this situation if you believe 'I must be treated fairly at work' because people at work haven't shown you that they have treated you fairly (i.e. this is a threat for you), but you won't be anxious about it if you believe 'I must not be treated unfairly at work' because people at work haven't treated you unfairly (i.e. this isn't a threat for you). So give careful thought about which of these two forms best reflects each of your non-ego GABs.

2 Non-ego general anxiety-related beliefs vary with respect to how general they are. For example, let's take one of the beliefs listed above: 'I must know that my loved ones are safe and I wouldn't be able to stand not knowing.' Let me now place this belief in a hierarchy that shows beliefs that are more general than it (placed above this belief) and less general than it (placed below this belief).

'I must know that everyone I know is safe and I wouldn't be able to stand not knowing'	More general ↑
'I must know that everybody who is significant to me is safe and I wouldn't be able to stand not knowing'	
<u>'I must know that my loved ones are safe and I wouldn't be able to stand not knowing'</u>	—
'I must know that my younger loved ones are safe and I wouldn't be able to stand not knowing'	
'I must know that my children are safe and I wouldn't be able to stand not knowing'	↓ Less general

As you can see, as we go up the hierarchy the belief contains fewer restrictions. Thus, in the top belief, the person demands that she must know that everyone she knows is safe, and so if she doubts the safety of one such person, she is anxious. Contrast this with the bottom belief, where the person demands that she must know that her children are safe and she is anxious only when she doubts their safety. Obviously, the person will experience anxiety far more frequently in the first case than in the second. Bear this point in mind as you formulate your general anxiety-related beliefs.

Formulate your alternative non-ego general concern-related belief

The next step in dealing with your non-ego GABs is to formulate an alternative non-ego general concern-related belief for each of them. These alternative beliefs are known as non-ego GCBs. If you recall from Chapter 2, the healthy alternatives to demanding beliefs, awfulizing beliefs and low frustration tolerance (LFT) beliefs are known as full preferences, anti-awfulizing beliefs and high frustration tolerance (HFT) beliefs. You will need to include a full preference and either an anti-awfulizing belief or an HFT belief when you formulate your non-ego GCBs. Here are the alternative non-ego general concern-related beliefs to those non-ego general anxiety-related beliefs listed above.

- I don't want to be late for appointments, but there is no law decreeing that I must not be late. If I were to be late, it would be bad, but not terrible.
- I'd prefer not being uncomfortable when talking to people, but I am not exempt from being uncomfortable under these circumstances. If I were to be, it would be difficult to tolerate, but it would not be unbearable and it would be worth bearing.
- It would be much better for me not to become anxious when I am in enclosed spaces, but there is no reason why I must not experience such anxiety. If I do, it would be hard to tolerate, but I could do so and it would be worth tolerating.
- I don't want to lose any of my valuable possessions, but this doesn't mean that I must not. If I do it would be a misfortune, but it wouldn't be horrible.
- It would be desirable for me not to be treated unfairly at work, but this is not a necessity. If I were to be treated unfairly at work it would not be good, but hardly awful.
- I really don't want to lose control of my thoughts, but I am not immune from so doing. If I do lose such control, it would be a struggle to bear, but I could definitely bear it and it would be in my interests to do so.
- I much prefer knowing that my loved ones are safe, but I don't need to know this. Not knowing this would be hard to stand, but I could do so and it would be worth it to me to do just this.

- I don't want there to be a possibility that I might get cancer, but that doesn't mean that I must have this immunity. If there were a chance that I might get cancer it would be hard for me to bear this, but I could do so. Also, it would be in my best interests to bear this possibility.
- I want my parents to be here to look after me, but they don't have to be. If they're not, that would be very sad, but not the end of the world.
- I don't want family members to argue, but this doesn't mean that this must not happen. If they do argue, it would be hard for me to bear, but I could bear it and it is worth it to me to do so.

Question both sets of beliefs

The next step is for you to question both of these beliefs. While there are a number of ways in which you can do this, I suggest that you do so by considering both your non-ego GAB and your non-ego GCB at the same time and by answering three questions. Let me first list these questions and then illustrate their use.

Question 1: Which of these two beliefs is true and which is false? Give reasons for your answer.
Question 2: Which of these two beliefs is logical and which is illogical? Give reasons for your answer.
Question 3: Which of these two beliefs yields largely healthy results and which yields largely unhealthy results? Give reasons for your answer.

I have discussed why anxiety-related beliefs (in this case comprising demands, awfulizing beliefs and LFT beliefs) are false, illogical and largely unconstructive, in Chapter 1, and why concern-related beliefs (in this case comprising full preference beliefs, anti-awfulizing and HFT beliefs) are true, logical and largely constructive, in Chapter 2, and I suggest that you review this material before proceeding.

In the following example, I will show you how Martha questioned her non-ego GAB ('I must know that my loved ones are safe and I wouldn't be able to stand not knowing') and her alternative non-ego GCB ('I much prefer knowing that my loved ones are safe, but I don't need to know this. Not knowing this would be hard to stand, but I could do so and it would be worth it to me to do just this') using the above three questions.

Martha's non-ego GAB

I must know that my loved ones are safe and I wouldn't be able to stand not knowing.

Martha's non-ego GCB

I much prefer knowing that my loved ones are safe, but I don't need to know this. Not knowing this would be hard to stand, but I could do so and it would be worth it for me to do just this.

Question 1: Which of these two beliefs is true and which is false? Give reasons for your answer.

Answer 1: My non-ego GCB is true and my non-ego GAB is false. Let me first compare the demanding component of my non-ego GAB with the full preference component of my non-ego GCB. If the demanding component were true, i.e. that I must know that my loved ones are safe, then not knowing this would not be a possibility because it would mean going against that law of nature. It is obvious that no such law exists because it is perfectly possible for me not to know that my loved ones are safe. I'd rather know this, that's true, but that doesn't mean that I have to know it. What I want doesn't have to exist in the universe no matter how much I want it. Thus, from what I have just said, I am not exempt from being uncertain about the safe whereabouts of my loved ones. So, the full preference component of my non-ego GCB is true.

Now let me compare the LFT component of my non-ego GAB with the HFT component of my non-ego GCB. It is not true to say that I wouldn't be able to stand not knowing that my loved ones are safe. If it were true then I would die or disintegrate whenever I didn't know that my loved ones were safe – this is rubbish because I am still alive and haven't disintegrated even though I have falsely told myself that I couldn't stand not knowing the safe whereabouts of my loved ones. Also, if my LFT belief were true, then I would forfeit any chance of future happiness if I didn't know that my loved ones were safe. Obviously this is false because I would not lose my capacity for happiness if I did not know that my loved ones were safe. I could be in doubt and still experience happiness in the future.

My non-ego GCB is true because I can prove that all five parts are true. Thus it is true that:

1 I want to know that my loved ones are safe – this is my desire and if I want something then it is true that I want it.

2 I don't have to know that they are safe – see above: it is patently not true to say that because I want 'X' therefore it is true that I must get 'X'.

3 It would be hard to stand not knowing that my loved ones were safe – since I care for my loved ones and would want to know (but don't have to know) that they were safe, then it follows that it would be hard to stand not knowing about their safe whereabouts.

4 I could stand not knowing that they were safe – see above: I would not die, disintegrate or lose the capacity for happiness.

5 It is worth standing not knowing that they are safe because doing so will get me over my anxiety problem and it is definitely in my interests to do this.

For all these reasons, my non-ego GAB is false and my non-ego GCB is true.

Question 2: Which of these two beliefs is logical and which is illogical? Give reasons for your answer.
Answer 2: My non-ego GAB is illogical and my non-ego GCB belief is logical. These two beliefs have two components and I will answer this question by considering these components one at a time. Let me first consider the demanding component and the full preference component. Both of these components are based on a partial preference, i.e. 'I want to know that my loved ones are safe.' This belief is flexible.

Now, my full preference belief both asserts what I want (i.e. 'I much prefer knowing that my loved ones are safe . . .') and negates my demand ('. . . but I am not exempt from not knowing this'). Both of these belief elements are flexible and are therefore logically connected together. Therefore, the full preference component of my non-ego GCB is logical. My demand, however, asserts both what I want to happen (i.e. 'I much prefer knowing that my loved ones are safe . . .') and my demand ('. . . therefore I must know this'). The first element of this demanding belief is flexible and the second is rigid. Therefore, my demanding belief is illogical because it contains an illogical non sequitur, in that you cannot logically derive something rigid from something flexible.

I recommend that you show this diagrammatically. Figure 2 shows what Martha's diagram looked like.

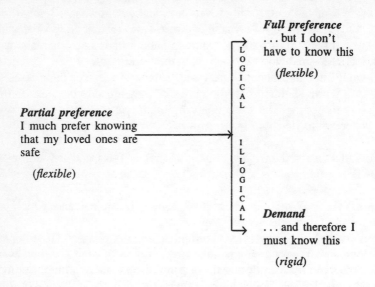

Figure 2

Now let me consider the LFT component and the HFT component. Both of these components are based on what can be called a partial HFT belief, i.e. 'Not knowing that my loved ones are safe is hard to stand.' This belief is non-extreme.

Now, my full HFT belief both asserts that not knowing that my loved ones are safe would be hard to stand and negates my LFT belief ('. . . but I could do so . . .'). Both of these belief elements are non-extreme and therefore logically connected together. Therefore, the HFT component of my non-ego GCB is logical. My LFT belief, however, asserts both that not knowing that my loved ones are safe would be hard to stand and that it cannot be stood. The first element of this LFT belief is non-extreme and the second is extreme. Therefore, my LFT belief is illogical because it contains an illogical non sequitur, in that you cannot logically derive something extreme from something non-extreme.

Diagrammatically, this argument appears as in Figure 3.

102

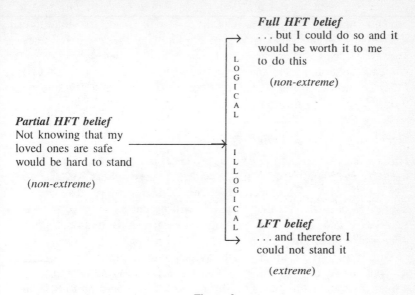

Figure 3

Question 3: Which of these two beliefs yields largely healthy results and which yields largely unhealthy results? Give reasons for your answer.

Answer 3: My non-ego GAB is largely unconstructive and will mainly give me poor results. Thus, when my loved ones are late, it will lead me to focus on the threatening aspects of the situation, e.g. that something bad may have happened to them. It will lead me to feel anxious about the whereabouts of my loved ones and it will influence for the worse my behaviour in these situations, e.g. it will lead me to check constantly whether they are coming up the road. Finally, it will lead me to think of the dire consequences of not knowing that my loved ones are safe, e.g. I may get images of bad road accidents happening to them and images of myself falling apart.

My non-ego GCB is, however, largely constructive and will mainly give me good results. Thus, when my loved ones are late, it will lead me to focus on the objective aspects of the situation and will only lead me to think that I am facing threat if, objectively, I am – e.g. that I hear that something has happened to my loved ones. It will lead me to feel concerned about their lateness when I am facing a realistic threat and it will influence for the better my behaviour in these situations – e.g. I will not check for their whereabouts; rather, I will get on with what I am doing unless they are very late and I haven't heard from them. Finally, it will lead me to think realistically of the consequences of not knowing that my loved ones are safe. Thus, I will not assume that uncertainty means threat; rather it means uncertainty. The constructive consequences of the non-ego GCB is summed up in its last component (i.e. '. . . and it would be worth it to me to do this').

Decide which set of beliefs you want to live by

Having questioned both your non-ego GAB and your non-ego GCB, the next stage is for you to decide which of these beliefs you wish to live by. If you have questioned your beliefs comprehensively, it should be clear to you that your life will be enriched by your non-ego GCB and hampered by your non-ego GAB and that your decision is clear cut.

However, it may be that you are reluctant to commit yourself fully to your non-ego GCB because you have some objections to it or some reservations/doubts about living your life according to it. You may also consider that your non-ego GAB has some advantages that you may lose if you commit yourself to your non-ego GCB or that there are negative consequences to adopting the non-ego GCB. If any of these are the case, then it is important for you to be clear with yourself about what these objections, reservations, doubts, losses and negative consequences are so that you can determine whether they are realistic or distorted.

Here is a list of Martha's objections, etc., and how she responded to them.

1 *If I commit myself to my non-ego GCB then I will increase the chances that something bad will happen to my loved ones*
Response: This is superstitious nonsense because I am saying that my beliefs have a bearing on what happens to my loved ones. This is obviously not the case. Adopting my non-ego GCB will neither increase nor decrease the chances that bad things will happen to my loved ones if I don't know that they are safe.

2 *If I give up my non-ego GAB then it means that I don't care about my loved ones*
Response: If I give up my non-ego GAB and replace it with an attitude of indifference then I may not care about my loved ones. However, if I replace it with my non-ego GCB then I will still

care about the safety of my loved ones without being anxiously preoccupied about it.

3 *Committing myself to my non-ego GCB will mean that I will fall apart with stress*
Response: Quite the opposite. My non-ego GCB will help me to be healthily concerned about not hearing about the safety of my loved ones. It is my non-ego GAB that leads to stress.

In this way, Martha dealt with all her obstacles, etc., about committing herself to her non-ego GCB, which she duly did. In the same way, after you have questioned both your non-ego GAB and non-ego GCB, identify and deal with the perceived obstacles, doubts, reservations, losses and costs that you associate with giving up the former and committing yourself to the latter. When you have done so, you are ready for the next step in your overcoming anxiety programme.

Before I go on to describe this step I want to emphasize one important point. In order to change your non-ego GABs to non-ego GCBs you need to question both sets of beliefs repeatedly. I suggest that you do so 20 minutes a day, using the three questions listed above. Then spend some time responding to any doubts, reservations, etc., that you have about committing yourself to holding your non-ego GCBs. This repeated practice is a vital part of acquiring a concern-based philosophy and becoming more realistic in inferring the actual existence of threat.

Understand the relationship between threat and your general non-ego beliefs

In Chapters 1 and 2, I discussed the impact of holding general anxiety-related beliefs and concern-related beliefs on inferences of threat. Basically, I showed that when you bring your general anxiety-related beliefs to relevant situations, you tend to focus on the threatening aspects of the situation that are consistent with the content of the GABs, whereas when you bring your general concern-related beliefs to the same relevant situations, you are much more realistic in the inferences that you make about these situations and only consider that threat is imminent when it is objectively clear that it is.

Thus, after you have questioned your non-ego GAB and your non-ego GCB and have committed yourself to the latter, it is useful to be aware of the kinds of inferences that you are likely to make when holding each belief. Why? Because this will help you to view situations that you have previously seen as full of threat more realistically.

This is what happened when Martha did this:

Martha's non-ego GAB	**Martha's non-ego GCB**
I must know that my loved ones are safe and I wouldn't be able to stand not knowing.	I much prefer knowing that my loved ones are safe, but I don't need to know this. Not knowing this would be hard to stand, but I could do so and it would be worth it for me to do just this.

This belief leads me to infer

1 There is a very good chance that something bad will happen to them if I don't know that they are safe.
2 My loved ones are bound to be involved in any accidents that I hear about when I don't know that they are safe.

This belief leads me to infer

1 If I don't know that they are safe, they are probably safe unless there exists real evidence to the contrary.
2 If I don't know that they are safe and I hear about accidents, there is no evidence to suggest that my loved ones are involved in these accidents unless there exists real evidence to the contrary.

Having become aware of the effect of your non-ego GAB and your non-ego GCB on your inferences, it is important to apply this knowledge. Let me put this step into the overall context of dealing with one of your non-ego GABs.

Step 1 Identify your non-ego GAB and its healthy alternative (non-ego GCB).

Step 2 Question both beliefs.

Step 3 Commit yourself to your non-ego GCB, having dealt with any objections, reservations, etc., to so doing.

Step 4 Become aware of the impact of both of these beliefs on the inferences that you are likely to make about relevant situations.

Step 5 Once you have become aware of anxiety-based inferences, label them as such and challenge the non-ego GAB that underpins them.

(Every time Martha did not know that her loved ones were safe and began to focus on her anxiety-based inferences – listed on the left-hand side of the above diagram – she challenged her non-ego GAB.)

Step 6 Actively hold your non-ego GCB beliefs and focus on the inferences that stem from them.

(Martha then actively rehearsed her non-ego GCB and focused on the concern-based inferences – listed on the right-hand side of the above diagram.)

Step 7 If you need to challenge your anxiety-based inferences by asking and answering questions designed to assess how realistic the inferences are, here are some suggestions:

- How likely is it that . . . ?
- Would an objective jury agree that . . . ? If not, how would they view it?
- Am I viewing the situation realistically? If not, how can I view it more realistically?

It is important that you practise these steps regularly if you are to develop your non-ego GCBs and the realistic thinking about situations you have previously viewed as full of threat.

The major goal of the interventions that I have focused on in this section is to help you to develop healthy non-ego GCBs so that you can view relevant situations more realistically and are less likely to see threat where none objectively exists. In the next section, I will show you how you can overcome your anxiety in specific situations if you think (realistically or not) that threat is imminent.

Dealing with specific episodes of non-ego anxiety by changing your specific non-ego anxiety-related beliefs

If you develop general concern-based beliefs in relation to matters that do not impinge on your ego or self-esteem (i.e. non-ego GCBs), you will generally be more realistic in inferring the presence of imminent threat to non-ego aspects of your personal domain. However, even if you do this, at times you will still be anxious about specific threats either because your inference about facing threat is accurate or because you may still occasionally think you are facing threat when you are not. As I explained in Chapter 1, when you experience anxiety in specific situations this is because you hold a specific anxiety-related belief in that situation. In this section, then, I will show how you can overcome specific episodes of non-ego anxiety largely by changing your specific non-ego anxiety-related beliefs (non-ego SABs) to specific non-ego concern-related beliefs (non-ego SCBs). The first step in this process is to discover why you are feeling anxiety in the specific situation under consideration. You can do this by using REBT's famous ABC framework.

Using the ABC framework

When dealing with non-ego anxiety in specific situations, the best way to use the ABC framework is as follows:

Situation = A description of the situation in which you are anxious
A = Threat (what you find most threatening in the situation)
B = Specific unhealthy beliefs about A (in non-ego anxiety these are most likely to be a specific demanding belief and a specific awfulizing belief or specific LFT belief)
C (Emotional consequence of A×B) = Anxiety

Let me use Martha's case to illustrate:

Situation: I am expecting my two adult children for Sunday lunch and they are ten minutes late
A (Threat): I don't know that they are safe
B (Specific unhealthy belief): I must know that my two children are safe today and I can't bear not knowing this.
C (Emotional consequence of A×B): Anxiety

The most difficult part of understanding your specific non-ego anxiety is pinpointing the aspect of the situation that you find most threatening. If this is the case, you might find it helpful to ask yourself the following question:

'In this situation, what one thing would take my anxiety away?'

The opposite of this answer is what you are most anxious about in the specific situation under consideration. In some cases, you regard this event as something that will definitely or probably occur.

Thus, let's suppose that Martha knew that she was anxious when her two children were ten minutes late, but didn't know why. So she would ask herself the question: 'In this situation, what one thing would take my anxiety away?' Her answer was: 'Knowing that my children are safe'. Thus, Martha was most anxious about not knowing that her children were safe.

Once you have assessed the ABCs of your specific anxiety, you may be tempted to question A if it is distorted. However, at this stage it is important that you assume temporarily that A is true. This enables you to challenge and change the non-ego SAB which underpins your non-ego anxiety in the specific situation in question.

Question both sets of specific beliefs

After you have identified your non-ego SAB, it is important to formulate the specific non-ego concern-related alternative to this belief. This is known as your non-ego SCB. Then you can question these two beliefs in the same way as you questioned your non-ego GAB and non-ego GCB, i.e. at the same time, by answering the following three questions:

Question 1: Which of these two beliefs is true and which is false? Give reasons for your answer.
Question 2: Which of these two beliefs is logical and which is illogical? Give reasons for your answer.
Question 3: Which of these two beliefs yields largely healthy results and which yields largely unhealthy results? Give reasons for your answer.

Your answers should be similar to those that you gave when you questioned your general non-ego anxiety-related beliefs and your general non-ego concern-related beliefs, with one important exception. Your answers should be specific, since you are questioning specific healthy and unhealthy non-ego beliefs.

At the end of this questioning procedure it should be clear to you that your non-ego SAB is false, illogical and unhealthy while your non-ego SCB is true, logical and healthy, and that if you want to overcome your non-ego anxiety in the situation in question and to feel healthily concerned instead, then you need to adopt your non-ego SCB and relinquish your non-ego SAB. Once again, if you have any doubts or reservations about this, deal with them in the same way as you dealt with your doubts and reservations about relinquishing your general non-ego anxiety-related belief and adopting your general non-ego concern-related belief (see pp. 104–5).

Martha took her non-ego SAB ('I must know that my two adult children are safe and I can't stand not knowing this') and formulated the alternative non-ego SCB ('I want to know that my children are safe, but I don't need this knowledge now. It is difficult tolerating not knowing where they are, but I can tolerate not knowing and it is in my interests to do so'). She then questioned these beliefs and clearly saw that her non-ego SAB was false, illogical and unhelpful. Her one major reservation about committing herself to her non-ego SCB was that it might lead to her not caring about her adult children. However, she realized on reflection that this was unlikely because this belief stressed her strong desire to know that her children were safe, which meant that it was very unlikely that she would not care about the safety of her children.

In order to change your non-ego SABs to non-ego SCBs you need to question both sets of beliefs repeatedly. I suggest that you do so 20 minutes a day. First, imagine that you are about to face the specific threat at A, and once you have done this keep this clearly in mind as you question these specific beliefs using the three questions listed above. Then spend some time responding to any doubts, reservations, etc., that you have about committing yourself to holding your non-ego SCBs. This repeated practice is a vital part of overcoming your specific non-ego anxiety.

Question threat at A

Once you have challenged your non-ego SAB and have increased your conviction in your non-ego SCB, it is important that you go back and consider how realistic your threat-related inference is at A. You can do this by asking the same questions that I listed on p. 107. Here they are again:

- How likely is it that ... ?
- Would an objective jury agree that ... ? If not, how would they view it?
- Am I viewing the situation realistically? If not, how can I view it more realistically?

Martha asked herself these questions after questioning her specific beliefs about a different A: 'Something bad has happened to my husband because he is 15 minutes late' while holding her non-ego SCB. She took this threat at A, questioned it and realized three things: she was assuming that her inference that something bad had happened to her husband was a fact; this inference was determined by her non-ego GAB and SAB and was not necessarily a reflection of reality; and it was much more likely that his lateness was due to a harmless cause than a harmful one. These realizations helped Martha to reinterpret her inference at A, thus: 'Although something bad may have happened to my husband, it is much more likely that he has been delayed by non-dangerous factors.' Martha really saw that holding a non-ego GCB and a non-ego SCB lead to accurate inferences about threat, while holding a non-ego GAB and a non-ego SAB lead to overestimation of threat. It is very important that you learn this same lesson, and the best way of doing so is to first challenge your own non-ego GAB and non-ego SAB, replace them with an alternative non-ego GCB and an alternative non-ego SCB, and question your inference at A while holding this non-ego SCB.

Deal with thinking consequences of non-ego SABs

Questioning inferences while holding a non-ego SCB rather than a non-ego SAB is also particularly important when dealing with the thinking consequences of specific irrational beliefs. Indeed, it is more important to do this when questioning these thinking consequences than it is when questioning inferences at A, for inferences at A are perhaps more determined by non-ego GABs than by non-ego SABs, while thinking consequences of non-ego SABs, as the term makes clear, are largely determined by those SABs.

In Chapter 1, I showed that when you hold a specific anxiety-related belief about a specific threat then this belief will not only affect your emotion and behaviour, it will also influence the way you subsequently think about the situation you are facing in ways which increase the threat content. When you do not understand this, you tend to see these new increased threats as real and then bring your anxiety-related beliefs to these new As, with the result that your anxiety level is increased. This explains why people can 'work themselves into' an intense state of anxiety and panic. When this process occurs in non-ego anxiety, the thinking consequences of your non-ego SABs (which are the new increased threats) are likely to reflect the following:

111

1 even more negative behaviour on your part;
2 a sense of being exposed to increasing levels of non-ego threat;
3 even more negative practical consequences in line with 1 and 2.

Thus, once Martha's non-ego SAB about specific threat (i.e. not knowing that her children were safe in the specific situation under consideration) was activated, then she began to think in ways that elaborated the threat in her mind. Thus, she began to think that:

1 'They have been involved in an accident'
2 'They have been badly hurt in this accident'
3 'They will die from their injuries'
4 'If something happened to them I would fall apart'

There are four ways of dealing with these thinking consequences of non-ego SABs.

1 Label them as thinking consequences of a non-ego SAB and then challenge and change this belief. Then you can go back and evaluate how realistic these thoughts are (if you need to) using the questions that I listed on p. 107.
2 Recognize that they are a sign that your anxiety is beginning to get out of control and that you need to use the ABC framework to gain control and understand what you were anxious about in the first place. In particular, you might find it helpful to ask yourself the following question: 'In this situation, what one thing would take my anxiety away?' As I showed you earlier, the opposite of this answer is what you are most anxious about in the specific situation under consideration. This definite or probably occurring event constitutes the A in the ABC framework, anxiety constitutes the C, and this is all you need to identify your non-ego SAB which you then go on to question in the normal way.
3 Take one of these thinking consequences, treat it as an A and do another ABC assessment on it. Then identify and question your non-ego SAB before assessing how realistic the A is (as before).
4 Treat them as inferences (without necessarily challenging the underlying non-ego SAB) and ask yourself questions such as those that appear on p. 107.

Use imagery to change your non-ego SABs

So far I have suggested largely verbal means of questioning your non-ego SABs and non-ego SCBs with the purpose of changing the former to the latter. You can gain practice at changing your non-ego SABs by using your imagery modality. This technique is called rational-emotive imagery (REI) and I will now give you a set of instructions of how to use it and illustrate its use with reference to Martha's case. REI is best used to overcome specific episodes of anxiety and you need to have assessed such episodes using the ABC framework. You also should have had some experience in questioning your non-ego SABs and non-ego SCBs and have committed yourself to the latter.

Step 1 Vividly imagine the specific threat about which you are anxious.

(Martha imagined waiting for her adult children to arrive for Sunday lunch and them being ten minutes late. She particularly focused on the threat in this situation which was for her not knowing that her children were safe.)

Step 2 Briefly (for about 30 seconds) allow yourself to feel anxious and rehearse your non-ego SAB while imagining the threat.

(Martha rehearsed her non-ego SAB – 'I must know that my two children are safe today and I can't bear not knowing this' – and allowed herself to feel anxious for 30 seconds.)

Step 3 Change your non-ego SAB to your non-ego SCB while all the time vividly imagining the threat, and allow yourself to feel concerned but not anxious about it.

(Martha changed her non-ego SAB to her non-ego SCB – 'I want to know that my two children are safe today, but I don't need to know this. It is difficult for me to bear not knowing this, but I can do so and it is worth it to me to do this' – while vividly imagining herself waiting for her children and not knowing that they were safe.)

Step 4 Stay with the feeling of concern and the associated non-ego SCB while continuing to imagine the threat for ten minutes. Actively rehearse this belief if you find yourself getting anxious again.

(Martha did this.)

Step 5 Repeat Steps 1–4 formally three times a day for about 15 minutes on each occasion and at other times when you begin to think about the threat and begin to get anxious about it. Use your feelings of anxiety as a cue to practise REI.

(Martha also did this.)

You may be wondering why I suggest that you briefly allow yourself to feel anxious while practising REI. Surely, I hear you thinking, you don't need to practise feeling anxious about the specific threat under consideration. You know that you are good at doing that! This is, of course, true. But I suggest building this brief period of feeling anxious into the technique because it reflects reality. It is unrealistic to expect that you will not from now on become anxious about the specific threat in question. Quite the opposite. But I want you to see that you can use your anxiety as a signal or cue to rehearsing your non-ego SCB and that by doing this you can make yourself concerned about the threat rather than anxious about it.

Use coping imagery

The purpose of REI is to give you practice in your mind's eye of rehearsing your non-ego SCBs in the face of threats, so that you can be healthily concerned about these threats happening rather than anxious about their occurrence. It is also important that you practise rehearsing, again in your mind's eye, facing more favourable outcomes. There are two situations that I suggest you rehearse.

First, you can imagine the threat occurring and see yourself dealing productively with it in some way. Here, for example, Martha might picture herself being in a situation where she doesn't know that her loved ones are safe and see herself coping well with this, being somewhat concerned but getting on with things as she would if she did know that they were safe. It is important that you choose what would be a constructive response for you (from a long- as well as a short-term perspective) rather than accept what someone else views as constructive behaviour. This form of coping imagery is best practised after you have gained from using REI on dealing with the same threat. REI helps you respond constructively to the specific threat from an emotional standpoint, while this form of coping imagery helps you to respond constructively to the threat from a behavioural perspective.

The second form of coping imagery involves you imagining doing well in the same situation, with one major difference: the situation is non-threatening. Thus, when Martha used what might be called 'success imagery', she imagined herself preparing herself psychologically for the possibility that she did not know that her loved ones were safe. Then she imagined learning that they were safe. In doing this, Martha particularly rehearsed the notion that uncertainty is more often associated with non-threat than with threat. Success imagery should be practised *after* REI but should be given equal time. This is important because it aids you in developing your conviction in your non-ego GCB. Why? Because seeing yourself having success experiences reinforces the idea that threat is not inevitable in the situation under consideration (and related situations) unless there is clear evidence that such threat exists.

Act on your non-ego concern-related beliefs

So far, I have shown you how to change your general and specific non-ego anxiety-related beliefs using your ability to think and to image. These are important steps and not to be downplayed. However, if you do not act in ways that are consistent with your general and specific non-ego concern-related beliefs and inconsistent with your general and specific non-ego anxiety-related beliefs you will not develop the former and change the latter, and thus you will neither overcome your specific anxiety problem nor become less vulnerable to non-ego anxiety. So action is central to overcoming anxiety, action that does not reinforce anxiety-related beliefs but does reinforce concern-related beliefs.

Refrain from acting on your anxiety-related action tendencies and act on your concern-related tendencies instead

In Chapter 1, I discussed various behaviours that stem from anxiety-related beliefs. These behaviours have two major components: action tendencies which, as the term makes clear, involve experiencing an urge or a tendency to act in certain ways, and overt behaviours where you actually act on these urges or tendencies.

As I stressed earlier in this chapter, when you experience non-ego anxiety it is important to view this as a signal to do something about it. In fact, when you feel non-ego anxiety you have a choice: you can decide either to act on your action tendencies (which I shall list presently) or to challenge the non-ego anxiety-related beliefs which underpin your non-ego anxiety. Of course, I recommend that you do the latter rather than the former, even though it is much easier to do the former than the latter, and the former gets rid of feelings of non-ego anxiety more quickly than the latter. However, I hope you have grasped by now that getting rid of your non-ego anxiety feelings in the short term is not the same as overcoming your non-ego anxiety in the longer term. Indeed, if you act on the following anxiety-based action tendencies in the short term, you make it harder to overcome your non-ego anxiety in the longer term because you strengthen rather than challenge your specific and general non-ego anxiety-related beliefs. What do you need to do instead? After you have challenged your anxiety-related beliefs and committed yourself to the alternative concern-related beliefs, you need to translate your concern-based action tendencies into actual behaviour. In particular:

1 Refrain from avoiding situations that you find threatening. Instead, get into the mind-set of your non-ego SCB and confront the situation

If you do this, two things will happen:

• if the threat materializes you will gain the experience of thinking rationally about it (i.e. viewing it from the perspective of your non-ego SCB) and of acting constructively as a result;
• if the threat doesn't materialize you will still have gained the experience of thinking rationally in case it occurred, and you will have realized that your inference of threat was unrealistic.

You do need to be sensible in confronting threat. Confronting too much threat too soon may not be good for you because you may not be able to use your developing self-help skills in such 'overwhelming' situations. On the other hand, going too slowly in confronting threat may reinforce your unhealthy and unrealistic view that you are fragile and need protection from a harsh world. For these reasons I normally suggest that when you confront threat, you do so according to a principle I have called 'challenging, but not overwhelming'. This involves you developing a hierarchy of situations that you find threatening, from the smallest threat at the bottom to the biggest at the top. You then confront the threat that you find a challenge, but not one that you would find 'overwhelming' at that time, nor one that you would not find a challenge to face. If you apply this principle and practise your non-ego SCBs as you do so, you will find that you make reasonably quick progress up your hierarchy of threatening situations. There are exceptions to this 'challenging, but not overwhelming', as in the treatment of phobias and post-traumatic stress disorder, but these fall outside the scope of this book. If you have a phobia or think you may be suffering from PTSD, in the first instance see your doctor who will, if necessary, make a specialist referral.

2 Don't withdraw from threat. Stay in the situation and think rationally and act constructively

If you withdraw from a situation because you think that a threat is imminent, you may again find temporary relief from your anxiety, but you will not overcome your anxiety in the longer term. This is true for two reasons. First, when you withdraw you are reinforcing your non-ego SAB, and second, you do not test your inference that a threat is imminent.

3 Relinquish your safety-seeking behaviours and focus your attention on the part of the situation where you anticipate threat

In Chapter 1, I discussed the concept of safety-seeking behaviours and how these help you deal with your anxiety in the short term but do not help you to overcome your anxiety in the longer term. In non-ego anxiety, the purpose of safety-seeking behaviours is, as the term implies, to help keep you safe from threat while remaining in the situation.

Perhaps the most common form of safety-seeking behaviour in non-ego anxiety is checking. Here, you act in repetitive ways to try to get information that the threat that you fear does not exist. In Martha's case, this would involve looking frequently up the road to see if her loved ones were about to arrive and telephoning their mobile phones to find out that they were safe. In doing this, Martha is reinforcing her non-ego SAB (it is as if Martha is saying: 'Since I must know that my loved ones are safe, I have to keep checking on their whereabouts when I don't know that they are safe'). Also, by using this safety-seeking behaviour, Martha deprives herself of the opportunity of seeing how realistic her inference is. Thus, when her inference is: 'If I don't know that my children are safe then something bad has happened to them', by checking and finding out that they are OK Martha does not get the experience of seeing that they can be OK if she does not check and that her uncertainty about their safety does not have to mean that something bad has happened to them. In these two ways, Martha unwittingly perpetuates her non-ego anxiety problem and deprives herself of the opportunity of working to overcome it.

What should Martha do instead? She should hold her non-ego SCB and refrain from checking to ascertain that her loved ones are safe until it is reasonable for her to do so. If she is in doubt concerning what constitutes 'reasonable' in such situations, she should ask herself the question: 'What would any person who is healthily concerned but not unhealthily anxious about the safety of their loved ones do in this situation?' and act accordingly. Instead of checking, she should act as she would act if she knew that her loved ones were safe (e.g. continue to read, watch TV, etc.) without checking.

In general, it is important to avoid using safety-seeking behaviours and instead to focus your attention on the situation where you think that threat may be present. As you do this, make sure that you do so from the perspective of your non-ego SCB, so that you get practice at thinking rationally about the possible existence of the threat and at viewing the part of the situation where the threat may exist realistically.

4 Stop seeking reassurance. Instead, start living with uncertainty, challenge your anxiety-related beliefs and be realistic in your inferences

When you are anxious about your health, for example, you may ask others for reassurance that the symptom you are anxious about is benign. If you receive such reassurance, you feel better for a while (because the threat has been removed, albeit temporarily), but you do not get over your non-ego anxiety because you still hold a general and specific non-ego anxiety-related belief about your health. These beliefs will then lead you to infer that you are ill if your symptom does not clear up very quickly and then, because you are anxious, you seek reassurance and the entire reassurance cycle is repeated.

What should you do instead of seeking reassurance? As in other cases, I recommend that you put up with the uncertainty of not knowing for sure that the symptom is benign and challenge your non-ego GABs and non-ego SABs about such uncertainty. Your non-ego GCBs and non-ego SCBs will then help you to be realistic in your inferences about your symptom and what it may mean for your health. This will then lead you to be more realistic and healthy in your reassurance-seeking; in particular, you will wait a reasonable amount of time before seeking medical advice (i.e. as evidenced by people who have a healthy attitude about their health), you will digest the information you are given and, if you are reassured, you will not go off and get a second opinion until it is reasonable for you to do so. Finally, you will not seek reassurance from those not qualified to give it.

5 Don't overcompensate in your behaviour, but do take sensible action

The purpose of compensatory behaviour in dealing with non-ego anxiety is often to prove to yourself that you can cope with great fear. Lawrence panicked whenever he felt out of control. He overcompensated for his anxiety by putting himself in situations

118

where he would feel very out of control. He did this to prove to himself that he could cope with his fear. If you share Lawrence's problem it is important that you tackle your anxiety problem in a gradual manner. Going at it like a bull in a china shop will only serve to reinforce your anxiety problem.

Instead of overcompensating for your non-ego anxiety, challenge your non-ego anxiety-related beliefs, commit yourself to holding non-ego concern-related beliefs and take sensible action, which in Lawrence's case would be to tackle his fear of losing control in a sensible, graded fashion.

6 Stop acting impulsively to neutralize the threat and give yourself time to think in a reflective, considered manner

When you hold non-ego anxiety-related beliefs and you think that a threat to your non-ego personal domain is imminent, then you may well act very quickly to get rid of the threat. Such impulsive behaviour is likely to make matters worse because it is based on an absence of considered, reflective thinking. Such thinking allows you to consider the options that are available to you, to think of the pros and cons of each course of action and to choose the best course available to you. However, in order for you to do this, you have to view the situation from the perspective of your non-ego concern-related beliefs.

As you have probably gathered, I recommend the combined use of non-ego concern-related thinking and concern-based action as a powerful way of overcoming impulsive action. Some people say that they don't have the time to question their beliefs in the heat of the moment. This is a valid point. Consequently, I suggest that you write down your non-ego concern-related beliefs on 3×5 cards (one to a card) and rehearse them frequently even if you are not facing threat. In particular, consult these cue cards when you think threat is imminent. Two of Martha's cue cards read: 'I don't need to know all the time that my loved ones are safe. I can stand not knowing and not checking' and 'Being uncertain about the safe whereabouts of my loved ones is hard to bear, but can be borne. Doing so helps me to learn that there is nothing intrinsically threatening about uncertainty.' Cue cards are frequently (but not always) shortened versions of fully expressed non-ego concern-related beliefs, but reflect the full meaning of the longer version.

Deal with your unproductive thinking strategies

The final issue that I wish to consider in this chapter concerns the importance of refraining from using unproductive thinking strategies in dealing with your anxiety. In Chapter 1, I showed you that in order to stop yourself from becoming anxious when you suspect that a threat is on the horizon, or to get rid of your anxious feelings once you have begun to experience them, you may use one or more of a number of unproductive thinking strategies, such as distraction, reassurance thinking, compensatory thinking and defensive thinking (see Chapter 1 for a full discussion of these unproductive strategies).

Instead of distracting yourself from threat to non-ego aspects of your personal domain, reassuring yourself that such a threat does not exist, thinking how tough you are (compensatory thinking) or defending yourself from the threat, it is important that you:

1 assume temporarily that the non-ego threat does exist;
2 acknowledge that you feel non-ego anxiety about this threat and use this as a cue to Step 3;
3 identify, challenge and change the non-ego SAB and replace it with your alternative non-ego SCB;
4 take appropriate action to strengthen your non-ego SCB as outlined in the previous section;
5 use problem-solving thinking in preparing to deal constructively with the threat (see Chapter 2, p. 58 for a discussion of problem-solving in dealing with threat);
6 put into practice your chosen strategy for dealing constructively with the threat.

In order to take these steps you have to first:

1 Become aware of your individual unproductive thinking strategies. Use the four general headings – distraction, reassurance thinking, compensatory thinking and defensive thinking – as a guide here.
2 Acknowledge that these strategies are unproductive, see clearly why this is so and resolve to give them up.
3 Realize that giving up these strategies involves you experiencing more non-ego anxiety in the short term, but that this is necessary if you are to overcome your non-ego anxiety in the longer term. This is so because you are facing up to the threat rather than

avoiding thinking about it or neutralizing it. Remember the point that an avoided or neutralized threat is an undealt-with threat.

In the next chapter, I will consider the situation where ego anxiety and non-ego anxiety interact and suggest what you can do constructively when this happens.

5
When You Have Both Types of Anxiety

In the previous two chapters, I discussed how to overcome both ego anxiety (Chapter 3) and non-ego anxiety (Chapter 4). If you read both chapters, you may have come to the conclusion that you suffer from either one type of anxiety or the other. While it may be true that your anxiety problems may be mainly ego in nature or mainly non-ego in nature, it may well be the case that both types may be present in your anxiety. If this is the case, there are two possible scenarios.

In the first scenario, you consider that you are facing two threats in the situation, one to your ego or self-esteem and the other to non-ego aspects of your personal domain. When this happens you need to decide which of these threats to deal with first, and when you have made your decision you need to stick with it until you have dealt with it before switching to deal with the other threat. It is important that you don't switch too soon from dealing with one threat to dealing with the other. Only make this switch once you have made sufficient progress in dealing with the first threat.

In the second scenario, you begin with one type of anxiety and then this anxiety serves as a trigger to your second type of anxiety. Here, the second type of anxiety would not exist if the first type did not exist, whereas this does not hold in the first scenario. Putting this diagrammatically we have Figure 4.

In this chapter, I will concentrate on the second scenario.

Ego anxiety about non-ego anxiety

When you have ego anxiety about non-ego anxiety, you begin by making yourself anxious about threats (actual or real) to non-ego aspects of your personal domain (see Chapter 4). Then you focus on your non-ego anxiety, and some aspect of this experience serves as a threat to your ego or self-esteem about which you make yourself ego anxious (see Chapter 3). Let me use the ABC framework to give you a few examples of ego anxiety about non-ego anxiety. In doing so, I will use the notation A1B1C1 to denote the original non-ego anxiety and A2B2C2 to denote the ego anxiety about the non-ego anxiety. In

Scenario 1

Situation

↙   ↘

Non-ego anxiety   Ego anxiety

Scenario 2

Situation

↓

Non-ego anxiety

↓

Ego anxiety

OR

Situation

↓

Ego anxiety

↓

Non-ego anxiety

Figure 4

these examples, I will detail the emotional, behavioural and thinking consequences at C of the original anxiety to show which aspect of C1 becomes the new A2. I will also suggest how to tackle each presented problem.

Geraldine

Situation: Riding on the underground thinking

A1 = 'The train may get stuck in the tunnel for ages and I will be trapped'

B1 = 'I must not be trapped in the train and if this happened I couldn't bear it'

C1 (Emotional) = Anxiety

    (Behavioural) = Avoidance of riding on the underground (if possible)

                    Only taking short journeys

    (Thinking) = 'I'll lose control of myself'

                    'I won't be able to breathe'

                    'People will see that I am falling apart'

$$\downarrow$$

A2 = 'People will see that I am falling apart'

B2 = 'I must appear in control to others in this situation and if I don't I am inadequate'

C2 = Anxiety

In this example, Geraldine's major problem is her original non-ego anxiety (because she has a well entrenched non-ego GAB about losing control), but the lesser of her problems (her ego anxiety) makes matters worse for her. In this situation, Geraldine needs to tackle her original non-ego anxiety problem first, using the approach and methods that I described in Chapter 4, and to devote most of her efforts to this end. Geraldine will need to switch her attention to dealing with this secondary ego anxiety (see Chapter 3) if it gets in the way of dealing with her original anxiety, before going back to dealing with the more serious non-ego anxiety.

Terry

Situation: Riding in a taxi which is about to go over a bridge
A1 = Thinking that I might have the thought of throwing myself off the bridge again
B1 = 'I must not think of throwing myself off the bridge and if I do, I couldn't stand it'
C1 (Emotional) = Anxiety
(Behavioural) = Distracting myself from the thought by whistling or humming
(Thinking)   = 'I may be going mad'

↓

A2 [having focused on the feelings of anxiety at C1] = 'This is a real weakness'
B2 = 'I must not have such a weakness and because I do this proves that I am a weak, pathetic person'
C2 = Marked increase in anxiety

In this example, Terry's major problem is his secondary ego anxiety, since he has an ego GAB about having weaknesses. This is reflected in the marked increase of anxiety at C2. If he didn't have this problem then he would still have the non-ego anxiety problem, but he would find it much easier to tackle. The existence of Terry's ego problem prevents him from tackling his original non-ego anxiety problem, and therefore he needs to deal with his ego anxiety problem first and devote most of his efforts to overcoming this problem (see Chapter 3). Once he has made strides at this, he can usefully address himself to dealing with his non-ego anxiety problem (see Chapter 4).

Non-ego anxiety about ego anxiety

When you have non-ego anxiety about ego anxiety, you begin by making yourself anxious about threats (actual or real) to your ego or your self-esteem (see Chapter 3). Then you focus on your ego anxiety, and some aspect of this experience serves as a threat to non-ego aspects of your personal domain about which you make yourself non-ego anxious (see Chapter 4). Let me again use the ABC framework to give you a few examples of non-ego anxiety about ego anxiety. In doing so, this time I will use the notation A1B1C1 to denote the original ego anxiety and A2B2C2 to denote the non-ego anxiety about the ego anxiety. In these examples, I will again detail the emotional, behavioural and thinking consequences at C of the original anxiety to show which aspect of C1 becomes the new A2. I will also suggest how to tackle each presented problem.

Bruce

Situation: About to go into an oral examination on his Master's dissertation

A1 = 'I may not be able to answer all the questions'

B1 = 'I must be able to answer all the questions that the committee asks me and if I don't then I am an idiot

C1 (Emotional) = Anxiety

(Behavioural) = Pacing up and down

(Thinking) = 'I may go blank'

A2 [focusing on my uneasy breathing] = 'I am losing control of my breathing'

B2 = 'I must control my breathing right now and I couldn't bear it if I don't'

C2 = Marked increase in anxiety

In this example, Bruce's major problem is his secondary non-ego anxiety, since he has a non-ego GAB about losing control of his physiological functioning. This is again reflected in the marked increase of anxiety at C2. If he didn't have this problem then he would still have the ego anxiety problem, but he would find it much easier to tackle. The existence of Bruce's non-ego problem prevents him from tackling his original ego anxiety problem, and therefore he needs to deal with his non-ego anxiety problem first and devote most of his efforts to overcoming this problem (see Chapter 4). Once he has made progress with this, he can usefully address himself to dealing with his ego anxiety problem (see Chapter 3).

Samantha

Situation: In the car with her boyfriend going to meet his parents

A1 = 'I may not have anything interesting to say and they may think I'm boring'

B1 = 'I must not bore my boyfriend's parents and if I do it proves that I am worthless'

C1 (Emotional)　　= Anxiety

　　(Behavioural)　= Asking boyfriend for reassurance that I am not boring

　　(Thinking)　　 = Image of boyfriend's parents looking bored and glancing at their watches

$$\downarrow$$

A2 = 'I'll feel uncomfortable'

B2 = 'I must feel comfortable on this occasion and it would be awful if I don't'

C2 = Anxiety

In this example, Samantha's major problem is her original ego anxiety (because she has a well-entrenched ego GAB about what other people think of her), but the lesser of her problems (her non-ego anxiety) makes matters worse for her. In this situation, Samantha needs to tackle her original ego anxiety problem first, using the approach and methods that I described in Chapter 3, and to devote most of her efforts to this end. Samantha will need to switch her attention to dealing with this secondary ego anxiety (see Chapter 4) if the presence of this secondary problem gets in the way of dealing with the original problem, before going back to dealing with the more serious ego anxiety.

Other complexities

As you may have already noted, in this chapter I have begun to show you some of the complexities of overcoming anxiety by discussing how to deal with ego anxiety about non-ego anxiety and with non-ego anxiety about ego anxiety. However, you may also experience ego anxiety about ego anxiety and non-ego anxiety about non-ego anxiety. In such situations, although the two anxieties exist in the same domain (ego or non-ego) they are different problems and should be treated as such. This means dealing with them one at a time rather than simultaneously. Let me give a brief example of each double-barrelled anxiety.

Ego anxiety about ego anxiety

Bernie made herself anxious about the possibility that her partner would show an interest in another woman at the social gathering to which they were travelling. If this happened, Bernie would consider herself worthless (a clear example of ego anxiety). Then, when Bernie began to be anxious about her partner's behaviour she also became anxious about her anxious reaction to his behaviour, because she saw this as a sign of immaturity which she hated herself for (ego anxiety about ego anxiety).

Non-ego anxiety about non-ego anxiety

Andy experienced non-ego anxiety whenever he was uncertain about other men possibly being aggressive to him (an example of non-ego anxiety). When he began to become anxious about such uncertainty, this served as a threat, in that he thought that he might lose control of himself, about which he became increasingly anxious (non-ego anxiety about non-ego anxiety).

Bringing order to chaos in overcoming complex anxiety problems

When your anxiety problem is complex (i.e. when you have either ego-anxiety about non-ego anxiety, non-ego anxiety about ego anxiety, ego anxiety about ego anxiety, or non-ego anxiety about non-ego anxiety) how can you tackle it in a way that brings order to the situation that may, if you are not careful, become chaotic? I have already made some suggestions about this issue earlier in this chapter, but let me now offer you a set of systematic guidelines in answer to this question. In doing so, I refer you back to Chapters 3 and 4.

1 Deal with one problem at a time
   • Don't try to deal with both anxieties at the same time. Rather, deal with one problem at a time.
2 Use one of the following points in selecting which problem to tackle first. Choose the point that you think will best help you overcome your anxiety problem in the long term.

- Choose to start with the problem that is the most anxiety-provoking for you. This is often the problem that stems from a well-entrenched (ego or non-ego) general anxiety-related belief.
- Choose to start with the problem that is most prevalent for you (if different from the above). Again, this is often the problem that stems from a strongly held ego or non-ego GAB.
- Choose to start with the problem the very existence of which will distract you from dealing constructively with the other problem.
- Choose to start with the problem that is easiest to tackle if you are feeling discouraged and require a boost to your confidence.

3 Once you have selected a problem to tackle first, stay with it, using the sequence of steps and techniques outlined in Chapters 3 and 4. Don't switch part way through to the other problem.

- This will help you to gain the most from the REBT approach to overcoming anxiety.
- It will stop you from getting confused.
- It will give you a sense of being in control. This is particularly important if you are anxious about losing control.

4 Once you consider that you have made sufficient progress on your first problem, switch to the second problem and work it through to the end by following the same sequence and using similar techniques as you did with the first problem.

Since overcoming complex anxiety problems is difficult you may require specialist help to do so effectively. Speak to your GP if you think that this might be the case for you.

This brings us to the end of the book. I hope you have found it of value and I wish you well in using the principles and methods that I have described. If you would like to drop me a line to tell me of your experiences in using this book to overcome your anxiety, please do so, c/o Sheldon Press. Thank you for your patience.

Index

distraction 27; ego specific
beliefs 82–4; problem-solving
57–8; reassurance 27–8; role
in escalating anxiety 25–7
threats: ABC framework 54–5;
activating events 22–7;
anxiety-related beliefs 13–16;
avoidance and withdrawal

87–9, 116–17; concern-related
46–50; ego and non-ego
16–20, 48–50, 76–9, 105–7;
facing 59–60; situations
anticipated 18

uncertainty 95